A Cott<
Halo:

Manchester and the Textile
Districts in 1849

Angus Bethune Reach,
ed. Chris Aspin

RP

Published by Royd Press
The Book Case
29 Market Street
Hebden Bridge
West Yorks.
HX7 6EU
www.bookcase.co.uk

First published by Helmshore Local History Society,
1972

This Royd Press edition, 2007

We are grateful to Stanley Challenger Graham for his
permission to use his transcription.

Cover picture: Views of Manchester (detail), C. W.
Clennell, 1857, Manchester Archives and Local Studies

We apologise in advance for any unintentional
omissions or errors, which we will be happy to correct in
future editions.

ISBN: 978-0-9556204-4-7

CONTENTS

ILLUSTRATIONS

From *Lancashire: the first industrial society* by Chris Aspin (1969), © C. Aspin:

pp. 11, 19: Manchester cellar dwellings in 1847, *The Pictorial Times*

p. 30: children in a mule-spinning room, from Fanny Trollope's *The Life and Adventures of Michael Armstrong*, 1840

p. 33: Manchester factory workers during the depression of 1847, *The Pictorial Times*

p. 67: the cotton mills of McConnel & Kenney in Union Street, 1829, *Lancashire Illustrated*

p. 116: the waterwheel of Ashworth's Mill at Egerton, from Tomlinson's *Useful Arts and Manufactures of Great Britain*, 1848

Manchester Archives and Local Studies, Central Library, Manchester:

Front cover: Views of Manchester, C. W. Clennell, 1857 (detail)

p. 71: Manchester Mechanics Institute, Cooper Street – moved to Princess Street after 1854.

p. 104: interior of the Free Trade Hall, Peter Street, 1865

p. 185, 1890s Manchester horse bus

From *The Pictorial History of Lancashire*, 1844

Back cover and p. 208: details from "The Power Loom Room" by Sly

p. v, Patricroft (Bridgewater Foundry) by Sargent

p. 32, mule room by Sly

p. 43: calico printing by Sly

p. 169, Middleton Church by Dodd

p. 52 "The Poor Child's Nurse" by William Newman, *Punch*, 1849, Lee Jackson's www.victorianlondon.org

p. 78: workhouse children, www.spartacus. schoolnet.co.uk

p. 125, John Wroe, http://www.utopia-britannica.org.uk/pages/John%20Wroe.htm

p. 136, Oldham from Glodwick, 1860, Hartley Bateson's *Centenary History of Oldham*, 1949

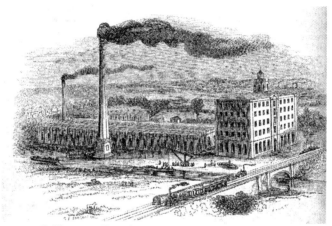

Bridgewater Foundry on the canal and railway, 1844

Reach's reports the same year on the Yorkshire textile districts are available in a companion volume entitled *Fabrics, Filth and Fairy Tents*, Royd Press, 2007

INTRODUCTION

"WE PUBLISH this day," announced the *Morning Chronicle* of October 18, 1849, "the first of a series of communications, in which it is proposed to give a full and detailed description of the moral, intellectual, material, and physical condition of the industrial poor throughout England." The undertaking, which continued until the end of the following year under the heading "Labour And The Poor," was described by a nineteenth-century historian of the English Press as "an unparalleled exploit in journalism";[1] and E. P. Thompson has said that the correspondents' reports form "the most impressive survey of labour and poverty at mid-century which exists".[2] But apart from the London section, which was the work of Henry Mayhew,[3] the project has been almost entirely forgotten.

The present volume is an edited version of the reports from Manchester and the surrounding textile districts published during October and November, 1849. Their author, Angus Bethune Reach (pronounced Reach), was a prolific journalist whose descriptive writing raised the reporter's craft to new heights during the middle years of the century. The son of an Inverness solicitor, Reach settled in London in 1841 at the age of 20 and won his spurs on the *Morning Chronicle*, for which he continued to work until illness ended his career in

---

[1] H. R. Fox Bourne, *English Newspapers*, 1887, ii, p. 154.

[2] E. P. Thompson and Eileen Yeo, *The Unknown Mayhew*, 1971, p. 23.

[3] The Survey was the starting point of Mayhew's *London Labour and London Poor*. Mayhew continued his investigations after leaving the *Morning Chronicle*.

1854. Charles Mackay, the poet and Reach's colleague on the newspaper, said of him:

> "In the capacity of a narrator of events which largely interested the public, he was constantly employed; and introduced a style till then unpractised, except in editorial articles, by means of which he brought before the reader's mind a vivid picture such as a novelist would paint, of every occurrence that passed under his eye – rapid, correct, graphic and full of life and animation. Under his influence the reader could see what he saw, hear what he heard and share all the emotions and excitement of the actual spectator of the scene. This was an immense advance upon the old reporting style. It immediately found imitators in other journals, and picturesque reporting became thenceforward the fashion."[1]

"No amount of work seemed too much for him," added Mackay, and another contemporary writer, George Sala, said it was no uncommon thing for Reach to work sixteen hours daily. He was therefore an ideal person to take part in the survey of 1849-50. He made a thorough investigation of conditions in the industrial districts, setting down his findings with admirable fluency and understanding in lengthy articles, two of which were published weekly during the early part of the undertaking. This would have been enough work for most men, but throughout his career on the *Morning Chronicle*, Reach contributed regularly to other newspapers and journals and found time to write novels and a number of humorous works. He also investigated

---

[1] Charles Mackay, *Forty Years' Recollections*, 1887, i, 150-151.

the condition of the wine growers and vineyard labourers of the Garonne, publishing his articles in 1852 under the title, *Claret and Olives*. Reach died in November, 1856, at the age of 35.

The *Morning Chronicle's* survey was prompted by the severe outbreak of cholera which focussed attention on the condition of the poor during the summer of 1849. "No man of feeling or reflection", said the newspaper in its introduction to the investigation,

> "can look abroad without being shocked and startled by the sight of enormous wealth and unbounded luxury, placed in direct juxtaposition with the lowest extremes of indigence and privation. Is this contrast a necessary result of the unalterable laws of nature, or simply the sure indication of an effete social system?"

In trying to find the answer, the newspaper certainly succeeded, as it predicted it would, "in making very valuable additions to the general stock of knowledge", and today the numerous articles are a rich source of information for both the national and local historian.

Reach began his survey in Manchester and also used the city as a base from which to make excursions to the surrounding districts. It was a particularly interesting moment for undertaking an inquiry into the condition of the poor. These were the closing months of a decade which had brought important changes in the country's financial and economic policies, in factory legislation and in the attitude of local authorities to health and sanitation. The 1840s had also seen a strengthening of voluntary help for the working classes, in particular that performed by the Sunday schools, and a gradual improvement of trade following the severe depression of 1841-44.

> The Manchester which I am describing [wrote Reach] is the Manchester of prosperous times. True, there has not been any recent fever of production; there has been no sudden and imperious demand for calicoes, such as in the olden times, before Ten Hour Bills were heard of, would have kept the steam-engines throbbing, and the mechanism whirling for fifteen or eighteen hours out of the twenty-four; but there has been for some time a fair and steady trade; the workpeople have for some time earned fair and steady wages, and the butcher and baker have happily had the power of being reasonable in their demands.

The ten-hour working day had been in operation a little over a year when Reach arrived in Manchester, but he found ample evidence of its benefits.

> I have personally conversed with at least two dozen young men and women who have learned to read and write since the passing of the Ten Hours Bill. Night schools for adults are now common; most of these have libraries attached to them. The men and boys learn reading, writing and cyphering; and the women and girls, in addition to these branches of education, are taught plain, and are in many instances teaching themselves fancy needlework.

These were some of the first fruits of reform; but as Reach observed, "Education is but yet opening its trenches and arranging its batteries. The social and sanitary pioneers have but just begun in earnest to advance." There was still much that shocked the visitor to Lancashire: squalid cellar dwellings, Oldham mills with their hot, unventilated rooms filled with flying dust, the drugging of young children whose mothers worked all day. It is an honest, impartial account that Reach gives.

Professor T. S. Ashton described the reports of the Royal Commissions and Committees of Inquiry as "one of the glories of the Victorian age. They signalised a quickening of social conscience and a sensitiveness to distress that had not been evident in any other period or in any other country." The Morning Chronicle's survey is a worthy companion to those investigations.

Reach wrote his descriptions of Manchester during and not at the end of his stay and he returned several times to topics discussed in earlier reports. I have therefore arranged the Manchester material under separate headings rather than giving it as it originally appeared.

Chris Aspin
Helmshore, 1972

MANCHESTER

1. "A thing of yesterday"

MOST ENGLISHMEN are, either from actual observation or reiterated description, familiar with the general appearance of what are called the manufacturing districts. The traveller by railway is made aware of his approach to the great northern seats of industry by the dull leaden coloured sky, tainted by thousands of ever-smoking chimneys, which broods over the distance. The stations along the line are more closely planted, showing that the country is more and more thickly peopled. Then, small manufacturing villages begin to appear, each consisting of two or three irregular streets clustered round the mill, as in former times cottages were clustered round the castle. Roads substantially paved with stone, so as to support the weight of heavy waggons, wind among the fields. Canals, with freights of barges, intersect the country; and the rivers, if they be not locked and dammed back, and embellished with towing paths upon the banks, run turbid and thick-charged with the foulness of the hundred mills they have aided in their course. Presently the tall chimneys begin to figure conspicuously in the landscape; the country loses its fresh rurality of appearance; grass looks brown and dry, and foliage stunted and smutty. The roads, and even the footpaths across the fields, are black with coal dust. Factories and mills raise their dingy masses everywhere around. Ponderous waggons, heavily laden with bales or casks, go clashing along. You shoot by town after town – the outlying satellites of the great cotton metropolis. They have all similar features – they are all little Manchesters. Huge, shapeless, unsightly mills, with their countless rows of windows, their towering shafts, their jets of waste steam continually puffing in panting gushes from the brown, grimy wall. Between these vast establishments, a network of mean but regular streets, unpicturesque and unadorned – just the sort of private houses you would expect in the vicinity of such public edifices; and around all this, and here and there scattered amongst all this, great irregular muddy spaces of waste ground, studded with black pools and swarming with dirty children. Some dozen or so miles so characterized, the distance of course more or less according to the point at which you enter the Queen of the cotton cities – and then, amid smoke and noise, and the hum of never-ceasing toil, you are borne over the roofs to the terminus platform. You stand in Manchester.

There is a smoky brown sky overhead – smoky brown streets all around – long piles of warehouses, many of them with pillared and stately fronts – great grimy mills, the leviathans of ugly architecture, with their smoke-pouring shafts. There are streets of all kinds – some with glittering shops and vast hotels, others grim and little frequented – formed of rows and stacks of warehouses; many mean and distressingly monotonous vistas of uniform brick houses. There are principal thoroughfares, busy and swarming as London central avenues – crowded at once with the evidences of wealth and commerce – gay carriages and phaetons – clumsy low-built omnibuses, conveying loads which a horse must shudder to contemplate – cars, carts and waggons of every construction, high piled with bales and boxes. There are crowds of busy pedestrians of every class which business creates – clerks and travellers and agents – bustling from counting-house to counting-house, and bank to bank. There are swarms of mechanics and artisans in their distinguishing fustian of factory operatives, in general undersized, sallow-looking men and of factory girls, somewhat stunted and pale, but smart and active looking, with dingy dresses and dark shawls, speckled with flakes of cotton-wool wreathed round their heads.

This city – this great capital of the weavers and spinners of the earth, the Manchester of the power-loom, the Manchester of the League,[1] our Manchester -is but a thing of yesterday. Sir Richard Arkwright was the man who laid the foundation of *our* Manchester. Since the introduction of roller-spinning the city sprang up as though by magic.[2] A man, only a very few years dead, recollected the people crowding to admire the first tall chimney built in Manchester, and had seen the Liverpool coach set forth at six in the morning, in good hope of its reaching its destination not very long after six o'clock at night. Considerably within two-thirds of a century the scattered villages of Manchester, Salford, Hulme, Pendleton, Chorlton and two or three others, became the vast cotton metropolis which has lately succeeded in swaying the industrial and commercial policy of England.

---

[1] The National Anti-Corn Law League, which was founded in Manchester in 1839. Its brilliant political campaign led to the passing of the Repeal Bill in 1846.
[2] Arkwright's spinning frame, patented in 1769, used pairs of rollers, revolving at successively faster speeds, to draw out the threads of cotton before they were twisted. Arkwright built Manchester's first cotton mill – a five-storey building, 200 feet long and 30 feet wide – in 1780.

2. Workers' Homes

MANCHESTER MAY be roughly divided into three great regions. The central of these – lying round the heart of the Exchange – is the grand district of warehouses and counting rooms. There the fabrics spun, wove, printed and dyed at the mills, are stored for inspection and purchase. There the actual business of buying and selling is carried on. There are banks, offices, agencies innumerable. The far outskirts of the city, again, form a sort of universally-stretching West-end. Thither fly all who can afford to live out of the smoke. There are open handsome squares, and showy ranges of crescents and rows, and miles of pleasant villas peeping out from their shrubberied grounds. Between these two regions – between the dull stacks of warehouses and the snug and airy dwellings of the suburbs – lies the great mass of smoky, dingy, sweltering and toiling Manchester. It is from that mid region that the tall chimneys chiefly spring, and it is beneath these – stretching in a network of inglorious-looking, but by no means universally miserable streets, from mill to mill, and from factory to factory – that we find the homes of the spinners and weavers, whose calicoes are spread abroad over three parts of the garment-wearing globe.

The streets of some districts are very far superior to those of others, although the inhabitants of all belong very much to the same class, and the rents paid are tolerably uniform. The old districts are, as might be expected, invariably the worst. They contain the largest proportion of cellar dwellings, of close, filthy courts, of undrained lanes, and of rows of houses built back to back, without any provision for ventilation, and with very little for cleanliness. Still, a tolerably extensive inspection of the worst localities of Manchester has not revealed to me alleys so utterly squalid and miserable as many I could name in London; and certainly the filthiest court which I have penetrated is decency itself compared to the typhus-smelling wynds and closes into which I have adventured in Glasgow. In the older parts of the borough of Manchester itself, along the great thoroughfare called the Oldham road, and in the Ancoats district – the latter entirely an operative colony – are situated some of the most squalid-looking streets, inhabited by swarms of the most squalid-looking people which I have seen. Outlying portions of the borough of Salford are also very miserable, full of streets unpaved, undrained, strewn with offal and refuse, and pierced with airless *culs-de-sac*, rendered still more noisome by the quantities of ill-coloured clothes hung to dry from window to window. The township of Chorlton – a more modern one – is decidedly better; but of all which I have yet seen – I am of course referring to the operative *quartiers* – the district Hulme (pronounced Hoom) presents the most cheering spectacle, not only on account of its comparatively broad and airy streets, but from the progress which it evinces in the plan of construction of the houses. Hulme is a new district. A very few years ago, a great portion of the space now covered with humble but comfortable streets was open fields.

The house of the Manchester operative, wherever it be – in the old district or in the new – in Ancoats or Cheetham or Hulme – is uniformly a two-story dwelling. Sometimes it is of fair dimensions, sometimes a line fourteen feet long would reach from the eaves to the ground. In the old localities there is, in all probability, a cellar beneath the house, sunk some four or five feet below the pavement, and occupied perhaps by a single poor old woman, or by a family, the heads of which are given to pretty regular alternation between their subterranean abode and the neighbouring wine-vaults.

Manchester cellar dwellings in 1847

In the modern and improved *quartiers*, the cellar retires modestly out of sight, and is put to a more legitimate use as a home for coals or lumber. Nothing struck me more, while visiting and comparing notes in the different operative districts of Manchester, than in the regularity with which the better style of furniture went together; it being always kept in mind that, so far as wages are concerned, the inhabitants of one locality are almost, if not quite, on a par with those of another. But the superior class room seemed, by a sort of natural sequence, to attract the superior class furniture. A fair proportion of what was deal in Ancoats was mahogany in Hulme. Yet the people of Hulme get no higher wages than the people of Ancoats. The secret is that they live in better built houses, and consequently take more pleasure and pride in their dwellings.

The worst class of houses, not being cellars, commonly inhabited by the "mill hands", consist each of two rooms, not a "but-and-a-ben", but an above and a below, the stair to the former leading directly up from the latter, and the door of the ground-floor parlour being also the door of the street. In some cases the higher story is divided into two small bedrooms, but in the superior class of houses there are generally two small, but comfortable rooms on the ground-floor, and two of corresponding size above. The street door in these tenements opens into a narrow passage, from which the stairs of the bedrooms also ascend. The window of the ground floor room, opening to the street, is always furnished with a pair of substantial outside shutters, and the threshold is elevated from the pavement, so as to admit of very emphatic stone door-steps with flourishing scrapers, both of which, by the way, are generally to be found in a very commendable state of purity. A local act of Parliament,[1] obtained a few years ago, and providing that every house built after its enactment in Manchester should be constructed so as to posses a back door opening into a small back yard, has been of immense advantage to the newer portions of the town. The unhealthy practice of building houses back to back was thus at once put down. A free current of air was permitted to circulate in the rear as well as in front of the tenements, and ample space was obtained for the necessary cesspools, ash-pits, &c., &c., while convenient

---

[1] For an account of public health and sanitary reform during the 1840s, see Arthur Redford and Ina S. Russell, *The History of Local Government in Manchester*, ii, 1940, p. 130f.

approaches for the cleansing of such receptacles from the back were everywhere formed. Take, for example, a part of Hulme, which I inspected the other day. Between every street were two rows of the best class of operatives' houses, each with four rooms and a cellar a-piece; and between each of the rows, running the whole length, was a paved courtway, with a gutter in the centre, formed by the back walls of the yards of the tenements on either side; the walls in question being pierced with apertures, through which all sorts of domestic refuse could be easily got at and conveyed away with as little annoyance to the inhabitants as may be. Certainly the plan was a vast improvement upon the old style of building. Still more might have been done. Most of the streets were provided with regular drains and gratings. In the case of new streets, I believe, the corporation insists upon these necessary appendages being completed within two years after the completion of the street (it would be as well, one would think, to make the whole business simultaneous); but the drains in question, as I am informed, only carry away the surface water and slops flung into the gutter in the central back passage, all sorts of foul refuse having to be removed by manual labour. The construction of water-closets is yet a desideratum, even in the best class of the operatives' houses; while in the old districts the accommodation in this respect is deficient in the extreme, and that which exists, filthy in the extreme. This is a matter which, in discussing seriously and earnestly the social condition of the people, it would be weak and foolish to shirk. There will be little female virtue where, in the very nature of things, there can be little delicacy or decent reserve. In town and in the country, in low lodging-houses, and in squalid clusters of agricultural cottages, the evil is the same. The sexes, at all times and at all hours, are huddled together, simply from want of room and accommodation to bestow them separately; and thus follow the inevitable results of brutalized men and hardened and shameless women – of childhood precociously knowing in everything which children ought not to know, and by consequence, precociously criminal.

I visited several of the better class houses in Hulme, and shall sketch in a few lines, the parlour of the first which I entered, and which may be taken as a fair specimen of the others. The room was about ten feet by eight, and hung with a paper of cheap quality and ordinary pattern. In at least two of the corners were cupboards of hard wood, painted mahogany fashion, and containing plates, teacups, saucers, &c. Upon the chimney-piece was ranged a set of old-fashioned glass and china ornaments. There was one framed print hanging from the wall – a steel engraving of small size, reduced from the well-known plate of the "Covenanter's Marriage." Beside this symbol of art was a token allegiance to science, in the shape of one of the old-fashioned tube barometers, not apparently in the most perfect state of order. There were two tables in the apartment – a round centre one of ordinary material, and a rather handsome mahogany Pembroke. Opposite the fireplace was one of those nondescript pieces of furniture which play a double part in domestic economy "a bed by night, a wardrobe all the day." The chairs were of the comfortable old-fashioned Windsor breed; and on the window-ledge were two or three flower-pots, feebly nourishing as many musty geraniums. The floor was carpetless – a feature, by the way, anything but characteristic. In the passage, however, was laid down a piece of faded and battered oil-cloth. The general aspect of the place, although by no means a miracle of neatness, was tolerably clean and comfortable. The landlady, a buxom dame of fifty, or thereabouts, does not work in the mill herself, but her sons and daughters – two of the latter married – all do. She was perfectly ready to submit her dwelling to our scrutiny, and expressed a strong hope, in anything which might be said of her or her family, that special mention might be made that "they were all for the Ten Hours Bill[1] in that house."

In the majority of streets inhabited by operatives the front room on the ground floor is used both as parlour and kitchen. Sometimes a second room of small dimensions opens back from it, and when such an apartment exists, it is generally seen littered with the coarser cooking and washing utensils. I have described the principal "public" room in a house of the first class in Hulme: let me sketch the generic features of the tenements in the older, worse built, and in all respects inferior quarter of Ancoats. Fancy, then, a wide-lying labyrinth of small dingy streets, narrow, unsunned courts terminating in gloomy *culs-de-sac*, and adorned with a central sloppy gutter. Every score or so of yards you catch sight of one of the second and third class mills, with its cinder-paved courtyard and its steaming engine-house. Shabby-looking chapels, here and there, rise with infinitesimal Gothic arches and ornaments, amid the grimy nakedness of the factories. Now a railroad, upon

---

[1] Following more than 15 years of agitation, the Ten Hours' Bill was passed on June 1, 1847. A month later it came into partial operation, with young persons (those aged between 13 and 18) and women restricted to 11 hours a day and 63 hours a week. From May 1, 1848, the hours were 10 daily and 58 a week.

its understructure of arches, passes over the roofs; anon, you cross a canal, with wharfs and coal-yards and clusters of unmoving barges. In most cases the doors of the houses stand hospitably open, and young children cluster over the thresholds and swarm out upon the pavement: you have thus an easy opportunity of noting the interiors as you pass along. They are, as you will perceive, a series of little rooms, about ten feet by eight, more or less, generally floored with brick or flagstones – materials which are, however, occasionally half concealed by strips of mats or faded carpeting. A substantial deal table stands in the centre of each apartment, and a few chairs, stools, and settles to match, are ranged around. Occasionally, a little table of mahogany is not wanting. Now and then you observe a curiously small sofa, hardly intended for a full grown man or woman to stretch their limbs upon; and about as often one side of the fireplace is taken up with a cradle. Sometimes there is a large cupboard, the open door of which reveals a shining assortment of plates and dishes; sometimes the humble dinner service is ranged on shelves which stretch along the walls; while beneath them are suspended upon hooks a more or less elaborate series of skillets, stewpans, and miscellaneous cooking and household matters. A conspicuous object is very frequently a painted and highly-glazed tea tray, upon which the firelight glints cheerily, and which, by its superior lustre and artistic boldness of design, commonly throws into the shade the couple or so of tiny prints, in narrow black frames, which are suspended above it. A favourite and no doubt useful article of furniture is a clock. No Manchester operative will be without one a moment longer than he can help. You see here and there, in the better class of houses, one of the old-fashioned metallic-faced eight-day clocks; but by far the most common article is the little Dutch machine, with its busy pendulum swinging openly and candidly before all the world. Add to this catalogue of the most important items of *incublement* an assortment of the usual odds and ends of household matters, deposited in corners or window-ledges or shelves – here a box, there a meal or flour barrel now and then a small mirror gleaming from the wall – now and then a row of smoke-browned little china and stoneware ornaments on the narrow chimney-piece – in general a muslin window-screen, or, perhaps dingy cotton curtains – and not unfrequently a pot or two of geraniums or fuchsias, rubbing their dry twigs and brown stunted leaves against the dim and small-paned lattice. Picture all these little household appliances, and others of a similar order, giving the small room a tolerably crowded appearance, and you will have a fair notion of the vast majority of the homes of the factory operatives, such as they appear in the older and less improved localities of Manchester. The cellars are, as might be expected, seldom furnished so well. They appear to possess none of the minor comforts, none of the little articles of ornament or fancy furniture which more or less you observe in the parlours. The floors seem damp and unwholesome, you catch a glimpse of a rickety-looking bed in a dark airless corner, and the fire upon the hearth is often cheerlessly small, smouldering amongst the unswept ashes.

Decidedly the worst feature of the house tenements is the (in some districts) invariable opening of the street-door into the parlour. One step takes you from the pavement to the shrine of the Penates. The occupant cannot open his door, or stand upon his threshold, without revealing the privacy of his room to all bypassers. This awkward mode of construction is objectionable in other respects, as tending, for example, to be a fruitful source of rheumatic and catarrh-bestowing draughts. But, as I have stated, the new houses are almost invariably furnished with a decent lobby, a characteristic which of itself places them fifty per cent above those built after the old fashion.

Saturday is generally the great weekly epoch of cleansing and setting things to rights in the houses of the Manchester workpeople. The last day of the week may, indeed, be generally set down as a half holiday amongst all the industrial population, exclusive of artisans and tradespeople. At the ordinary dinner hour, there is a vast stir amongst the denizens of counting houses and warehouses, many of whom have country establishments to visit upon the Saturday, and one o'clock sees a simultaneous starting of scores of heavily-laden omnibuses bound for every suburb and village of and round Manchester. The mills knock off work at about two or half after two o'clock, and if you visit the class of streets which I have been attempting to describe an hour or so thereafter, you will marvel and rejoice at the universality of the purification which is going forward. Children are staggering under pails and buckets of water, brought from the pump or the cock which probably supplies a small street. Glance in at the open portals, and you will witness a grand simultaneous system of scouring. The women, of course, are the principal operators – they are cleaning their windows, hearthstoning their lintels, scrubbing their furniture with might and main. The *pater familias*, however, does not always shirk his portion of the toil. Only last Saturday I came upon two or three lords of the creation usefully employed in blackleading their stoves.

Manchester cellar dwellings in 1847

Every evening after mill hours these streets, deserted as they are, except at meal times, during the day, present a scene of very considerable quiet enjoyment. The people all appear to be on the best terms with each other, and laugh and gossip from window to window, and door to door. The women, in particular, are fond of sitting in groups upon their thresholds sewing and knitting; the children sprawl about beside them, and there is the amount of sweethearting going forward which is naturally to be looked for under such circumstances. Certainly the setting of the picture is ugly and grim enough. A black, mean-looking street, with a black unadorned mill rising over the houses, and a black chimney pouring out volumes of black smoke upon all – these do not form very picturesque accessories to the scene, but still you are glad to see that, amid all the grime and dinginess of the place, there is no lack of homely comforts, good health, and good spirits.

The rents paid by the operatives in Manchester vary from 3s. to 4s. 6d., and in some cases 5s. per week. This is for an entire house. Cellar dwellings fetch – I give the statement upon the authority of Mr. P. H. Holland, surgeon, whose report upon the sanitary condition of Chorlton was published in 1844 – from 1s. to 2s. weekly, according to size. There is, however, I am happy to understand, upon all sides, a growing disinclination to those unwholesome abodes; but as their rent is low, a period of stagnation in trade often forces the people to occupy them. In 1844 Mr. Holland calculates that in Chorlton one cellar in every six was empty. The number of cellars, as compared with that of houses, was then one in twenty-eight. Mr. Holland adds, "They (the cellars) are much disliked, and justly so. They are always badly lighted and ventilated, and generally badly drained." In Chorlton Mr. Holland calculates that about one-third of the working population live in houses constructed back to back, and consequently without any thorough ventilation. About one-eighth live in "closed courts, or streets which are little better than courts." Now Chorlton being neither a very new nor a very old district, may be taken as giving not a bad idea of the general style of the working homes of Manchester. The proportion of people living in unventilated, undrained, and unwholesome buildings, in the districts traversed by the St. George's-road, the Oldham-road, and Great Ancoats-street, must be much more considerable, while in such districts as Hulme the case is reversed.

Manchester, like most great manufacturing and commercial cities, is scantily supplied with water, and that which is to be procured is not by any means universally transparent or tasteless. The streams which traverse the town are incarnations of watery filth. A more forbidding-looking flood than the Medlock, as it may be seen where it flows beneath the Oxford-road, it would be difficult to conceive. The black foetid water often glistens with the oily impurities which float upon its surface, and the wreathes and patches of green froth which tesselate it prove the effervescence produced by impure gases. For any household purposes whatever, the water of this uncovered sewer is quite out of the question; and the contents of the larger stream of the Irwell are not much better. Manchester, therefore, obtains its water partially by means of pipes, partially by means of wells and pumps. The last satisfactory statistics which have been published upon the subject are those contained in the "Manchester Police Returns," compiled by Captain Willis, the head of the constabulary force, for 1847. By these returns it appears that the number of "streets, squares, alleys, &c., within the borough of Manchester" was, at the date in question, 2,955. The number of dwelling houses was 46,922. Of these there were "supplied with pipe water in the interior, including shops," 11,190; while not less than 12,776 "houses, &c.," derived their water from a common cock or tap in the street. The number of houses which reaped no advantage, either from pipes conducted into their interiors, or from taps in the streets, was nearly as great as the amount of dwellings provided for in both of these ways, being 22,956. The number of dwelling-cellars in the borough was 5,070. Of these only 1,408 were provided with pipe water. Upwards of 1,968 had the advantage of a common tap, and 1,994 were entirely dependent upon other means of supply. The water sold by the Waterworks Company is derived from a tunnel called Gorton's Brook, which is principally land drainage. So intensely impure is the atmosphere over Manchester, that the rain water is unfit even for washing until it has stood some time to purify and settle. Many of the poor who have no cisterns to allow the water to rest in, and probably no room for them even if they had, carry the fluid to be used for washing and scouring from the canals, and are frequently so economic in their use of it that they keep a bucket-full until it stinks. Mr. Holland has "frequently detected the practice by the abominable smell produced in a patient's sick room". Generally the landlord of a set of houses sinks one or more wells, covering them of course with pumps, for the use of his tenants. The right to draw water from these sources is purchased by the neighbours at the rate of from 6d. to 1s. per quarter. Sometimes they come as far as a quarter of a mile to a favourite pump, or have the water carried home to them, paying for its conveyance a penny for every three gallons. Where standpipes or public taps are erected, the charge by the water company is about 10s. a year for every house the inmates of which use the convenience. Of the petty thefts which occur in Manchester, however, none – although they do not appear in the police returns – are so common as larcenies from taps and pumps. Many people, too, who do not choose to steal their water, obtain it merely as cheaply by begging for it. The "pressure" is kept on by the Waterworks Company for a few hours each day, Sunday excepted: and, consequently, cisterns and tanks are necessary when the quantity of water required for the day's consumption is at all large. In the course of a year or two, it is probable that Manchester will be bountifully and cheaply supplied with water. The works now in course of construction to conduct a fresh stream of the pure fluid from Glossop will, when completed, vie with many of the most superb aqueducts of antiquity.[1] I may add here, that the pumps attached to factories are frequently made use of by the workpeople. Messrs. Harvey and Tysoe[2] have sunk a well, for the use of which one penny per week is charged, the small sums thus collected going to the mill library fund, for the purchase of books. Another gentleman, Mr Ashton, a very extensive millowner at Hyde, has, at his own expense, introduced water into no less than 320 labourers' houses belonging to him, at the total cost of about £1 per tenement. The rent he charges for this convenience is the moderate sum of one shilling per annum — a weekly sum of three-pence being charged for the water itself. Since the introduction of this system, Mr Ashton informed the Health of Towns Commissioners that the houses, and especially the back-yards, were very much cleaner, and that the change was very observable in the persons of the people themselves. Mr Ashton is for a compulsory supply of water, to be introduced to every tenement, however humble. The system of taps or public pumps he describes as being fraught with all sorts of danger to morals.

Upon the whole, then, I am rather inclined to look hopefully upon the condition of the dwellings of the operatives of Manchester. At all events, there is an evident disposition to improvement. The corporation are rigid in enforcing the observance of the Local Building Act; and as Manchester is still rapidly increasing, the

---

[1] The Longdendale Aqueduct, which runs five and a half miles from Rhodeswood Reservoir to Godley, was built between 1847 and 1850.

[2] Reach visited Harvey and Tysoe's mill in Canal Street, Salford.

proportion of better class dwellings is becoming every day greater. I believe, too, that a very powerful stimulus has been given to increased neatness at home by the additional evening leisure time which the Ten Hours Bill has insured to the women. "I have time now to clean my house, and I do it, too, every evening" is the phrase I have heard repeated a hundred times by the tenters and female weavers. "Before, I was so tired that I could do nothing but just eat my supper and go to bed," they generally added. I fear, indeed, that anything like a thorough reform of that great portion of operative Manchester – built upon a bad plan, or rather upon no plan at all, save perhaps, that promising a yearly return of shillings in the pound – is at present out of the question. It is not, however, I know, beyond the powers of the people, if they be sober and industrious, to keep almost clear of the cellar dwellings. Building societies are a very common means of investing the savings of wages, and I believe that the people are beginning to see that the better the dwellings are, the cheaper in proportion can they be rented. For an additional third of what a cellar costs, a decent house, with several rooms and respectable conveniences, can be procured. The millowners in Manchester have paid, until recently, little or no attention to the state of the dwellings of their workpeople. They have maintained that if the labouring rooms in the factory were tolerably sweet and wholesome, that was all which they had to do with the matter: that the homes of their workmen and workwomen were the exclusive concern of the dwellers in them – a doctrine which, if not perfectly correct, was, at all events, exceedingly convenient. But the question comes to be, whether, in such a system as the factory one – a system in which an employer can exercise almost as great a degree of moral influence over great masses of the employed as the captain of a man-of-war can do over his crew at sea – whether, in such circumstances, the employer is not – morally at least, if not politico-economically – bound to attempt by his intelligence and enlightenment as much as possible to guide and direct the efforts and the energies of the new social development which he has himself aided in calling into being, and which is rising with so strange and anomalous a rapidity around him. It is to be presumed that all sorts of property confer their duties – mills, and steam-engines, and warehouses, and printed calico, as well as fields and woods; and if a landowner is not held to perform his duty unless he pays some attention to the social and sanitary state of the labourer upon his ground, so I cannot see that the manufacturer is to be excused from a similar obligation. That ideas of this class are now making way, both in field and city, I am happy to believe. Unhappily, the bulk of Manchester arose during a period in which they have had no existence – during which master and man more commonly regarded each other as mutual enemies rather than as mutual dependants, whose best interest it was to be mutual friends. A vast population suddenly sprung up round the mills. This population had to be housed, and they fell into the hands of unchecked speculators, who ran up mobs of filthy and inconvenient streets and courts, utterly unheeding, or perhaps profoundly ignorant of, the sanitary and social guilt of their doings.

3. The Mills

I HAVE visited and minutely inspected three cotton mills – two of them spinning establishments – one of them a spinning and weaving factory. These three mills I selected as likely to afford fair average specimens of the condition of the textile industry in Manchester. The first establishment which I visited was the great spinning and weaving factory of the Messrs. Birley, situated on the small stream of the Medlock, in the district of Chorlton-upon-Medlock. This establishment, including a manufactory of Macintosh cloth, which adjoins it, and which is the property of the partners, consists of several huge piles of buildings, separated from each other by streets, but connected by subterranean tunnels, in which iron tramways are laid down for the speedier and easier conveyance from ware-room to ware-room of the raw material. Nearly 2,000 hands are regularly employed in this vast industrial colony, and the machinery with which it is filled is impelled by several steam-engines, some of them of small power – a couple working with the strength of seventy, and one with the force of one hundred and fifty horses. Like the great majority of mills in Manchester, Messrs. Birley's establishment works fairly ten hours a day. The thread spun there is of the coarser quality, and is principally intended to be woven into cloth for the foreign markets, a statement which leads me to a general remark which must be constantly kept in mind in all our inquiries into the cotton-mill system. Manufactories of this species of fabric are divided into classes, according to the fineness of tenuity of the threads into which they spin the raw fibre of the cotton. The mills producing the most delicate threads – such, for example, as those requisite in the manufacture of lace – are called "fine-spinning mills." The motion of the machinery in these mills is slowest, and, as a general rule, the wages of the operatives are highest, the thread being more valuable, and a greater degree of care and attention being requisite for its production. There are, then, "fine" spinning mills, "coarse" spinning mills and a variety of establishments producing thread of intermediate degrees of fineness, which I may term medium mills. The factory of the Messrs. Birley spins, as I have said, coarse threads and the coarser ranges of the medium varieties. This factory has been long established, and being the largest in Manchester, may fairly be considered as one of the largest, if not the largest in the world. A former partner in the mill was one of the magistrates in command at the riot nicknamed Peterloo.[1]

A weaving shed in the 1840s

[1] Capt. Hugh Hornby Birley was one of the commanders of the Manchester and Salford Yeomanry at Peterloo (August 16, 1819). He died in 1845.

The second mill which I visited is a much smaller kind. It is situated in Canal-street, Oldfield-road, and has been driven by the same steam-engine for half a century. This factory is the property of Messrs. Harvey and Tysoe – gentlemen who exert themselves to the utmost to promote the social comfort and improvement of their workpeople. In the admirably ordered establishment which they possess are workmen who have toiled for the same masters for more than forty years; and twenty years ago, a spinner, who had been in the service of the same partners for thirty-two years, was carried to the grave by six of his comrades, who had laboured beside him for more than twenty years. This is a "fine" spinning mill. The partners are steady adherents of the teetotal system, and lose no opportunity of inculcating the advantages of temperance upon their workpeople. The hours of labour are ten.

The third mill which I have inspected is one of a medium size, and is spinning fine and medium thread, some of the former so exquisitely attenuated as to furnish more than 15,000 yards to the pound weight. Cotton, however, can be spun to a much greater fineness still. The factory at present in question is the property of Messrs. Gardner and Bazley, who are also the owners of a country mill.[1] Both of the mills work ten hours a day, according to act of Parliament.

In inspecting the two latter establishments which I have mentioned, every facility was afforded me for forming an accurate judgment of the condition of the workpeople. Messrs. Harvey and Tysoe laid their wages-book before me, and were at pains to educe the exact average of the earnings of their people. Mr. Bazley also

---

[1] Gardner and Bazley ran a mill in Water Street, Manchester, and another at Barrowbridge, near Bolton.

gave me every information as to the wages in every department of his establishment; and in both mills I was invited to put any question to the operatives which I might desire. This last privilege I was not slow of using. The workpeople conversed freely with me in the mills, and I have had ample opportunities in other quarters of holding personal conference with operatives of all grades in the cotton manufacture, and of all varieties of opinion, respecting the conditions under which it is, or ought to be, carried on.

Reach here describes at some length the jobs undertaken in a cotton mill. Of mule spinning, he writes:

This is the process in which there is most muscular exertion. That exertion, however, merely consists in walking. The distance thus traversed every day has been variously estimated. I remember Lord Ashley[1] used to find plenty of calculators who put it at a score of miles a day. More reasonable estimates vary from seven to eleven miles; and from the inquiries which I have made, and the rude calculations which I have been trying to frame, I should be inclined to put the distance as much nearer the former figure than the latter. Be the work what it may, however, the place of a spinner is one of the prizes of the cotton trade. The ordinary wages of this

---

[1] Lord Ashley, later 7th Earl of Shaftesbury (1801-85), was the Parliamentary leader of the factory reformers from 1833 until 1846. His statement that spinners walked more than 20 miles a day in working their mules was rejected by the mill masters, who put the distance at about eight miles. See Hansard, March 15, 1844, and Rhodes Boyson, The Ashworth Cotton Enterprise. Oxford, 1970, pp 181-2, for Ashley's dispute with the masters.

class of operative varies from £2 to £2 5s. and £2 10s. per week. His piecers[1] earn, say, on the average, 11s. per week, and the tiny scavenger clears his or her half-crown. The wives of the spinners never work in a mill; and this I believe to be a very strong incentive, over and above the high wages, to induce the men to struggle for the post; so at least they have told me over and over again. The spinner is quite a patron in his way. He employs his own piecers and his own scavenger, generally selecting the younger members of his family for both offices.

Children in a mule-spinning room, 1840

---

[1] Piecers – Children who joined the broken threads.

The operations of a cotton mill are really performed by machinery, and the workman does little but superintend the machinery, supply it with material, and remove that material when the mechanism has done its duty. Vigilant attention, and a greater or less proportion of manipulating dexterity – the degrees of either being exactly reflected by the amount of wages paid – are the great, indeed the only, requisites for the toil. That toil appears to me to be neither especially severe or irksome. The attention, indeed, is kept upon the stretch, but the faculty is not such a high one as, in the case of adults at least, to be very easily wearied, while the manual operations, every now and then requisite, are of that light and dexterous class which diversify the labour without fatiguing the labourer. The average of wages I have been at pains to ascertain. A very careful calculation, made from the books of Messrs. Harvey and Tysoe, gives as the result an average over men, women and young persons, of 11s. 3¾ d. weekly. This is probably a somewhat high average, as the mill spins fine, and children under thirteen years of age are not employed. In Messrs. Gardner and Bazley's factories, which spin rather coarser threads, the average is from 10s. 6d. to 11s. Taking then, all the mills, coarse and fine, now working at ten hours, according to Act of Parliament, I believe that I am justified in estimating the average wages at nearly 11s. per week. And here let us bear in mind that, in speaking of the average of wages, we are apt frequently to take the head of a family as the sole recipient, his household looking to him for support. Here the case is different. Take a man, his wife, and his children working in the mills, and the average wage is 11s. – not earned by one for the support of all, but earned by each for the support of each, or by all for the support of all.

A mule room in 1844

4. Mill Workers

I HAVE described the operations of a cotton mill, considered generally with reference to the operators. Let me now try to convey a correct idea of the operators themselves at their work. In the majority of mills labour begins at six o'clock a.m. throughout the year. In a certain number the engine during the dead winter months does not start until half an hour later. As a general thing, however, operative Manchester is up and stirring before six. The streets in the neighbourhood of the mills are thronged with men, women and children flocking to their labour. The girls generally keep in groups with their shawls twisted round their heads, and every few steps, in the immediate vicinity of the mill, parties are formed round the peripatetic establishments of hot coffee and cocoa vendors. The factory bell rings from five minutes before six until the hour strikes. Then – to the minute – the engine starts, and the day's work begins. Those who are behind six, be it but a moment, are fined two pence; and in many mills, after the expiration of a very short time of grace, the doors are locked, and the laggard, besides the fine, loses his morning work.

Manchester factory workers, 1847

Breakfast hour comes round at half past eight o'clock. The engine stops to the minute, and the streets are again crowded with those of the operatives who live close by the mills. A great many, however, take their breakfasts in the factory, which, as a general rule, supplies them with hot water. The practice of the people taking their meals in the mill, though I believe contrary to the letter of the law, is quite necessary, owing to the distance which many of the workpeople live from their place of labour, and to the short time – only half an hour – allowed for the meal. Its constituents are generally tea and coffee, with plenty of bread and butter, and in many cases a slice or so of bacon. At five minutes to nine the factory bell sounds again, and at nine the engine starts again. The work goes on with the most perfect method and order. There is little if any talking, and little disposition to talk. Everybody sets steadily and tranquilly about his or her duties, in that calm methodical style which betokens perfect acquaintance with the work to be done, and perfect skill wherewith to do it. There is no hurrying or panting and toiling after the machinery. Everything appears – in ordinary phrase – to be "taken easy"; yet everything goes rapidly and continuously on. The men commonly wear blue striped shirts, trowsers, and slippers the women generally envelop themselves in coarse pinafores and loose jackets tying round the throat. Spinners and piecers go about their work generally barefoot, or with such an apology for *chaussure* as forcibly reminds you of the old story of the sedan chair with the bottom out. Were it not for the honour of the thing, they might just as well go entirely unshod. I fear that I cannot say much for the cleanliness of the workpeople. They have an essentially greasy look, which makes me sometimes think that water would run off their skins as it does off a duck's back. In this respect the women are just as bad as the men. The spinners and piecers I have mentioned fling shoes and stockings aside, but I fear it is very seldom that their feet see the interior of a tub, with plenty of hot water and soap. The floor which they walk upon is as dark as the darkest Mahogany from the continued oily drippings with which it is anointed; and it is really painful to see a pretty girl with toes and ankles the exact colour of the dingy boards. Efforts have been made for the establishment of baths for the working classes in Manchester, and several millowners have actually erected conveniences of the sort, but the operatives in too many cases absolutely declined making use of them, and, as a general rule, can with very great difficulty, if at all, be made to appreciate the advantages of clean skin and free pores.

The atmosphere in which the work is conducted I found to vary very much in different mills. In the fine factories a higher temperature is requisite than in the coarse, and the old mills are generally built upon defective ventilating principles, or rather upon no ventilating principles at all. Very considerable attention, however, is paid in all the factories to keeping up a supply of pure air; the object being attained by scientific means in the newer mills, and aimed at through the medium of open windows and swinging panes in those of an earlier date. The atmosphere in Messrs. Gardner and Bazley's establishment was remarkably fresh and agreeable. Of course the air in which they work exercises a marked effect upon the appearance of the people. I do not remember seeing one male or female adult to whom I would apply the epithet of a "stout" man or woman. There is certainly no superfluity of flesh in the factories. When I say this, I do not by any means intend to insinuate that the people are unhealthy, or unnaturally lean; they are generally thin and spare, but not emaciated. By such occupation as is afforded in the various branches of cotton spinning, much muscle cannot be expected to be developed. There is no demand for it – the toil does not require it – it would be useless if it existed. I cannot, therefore, term the appearance of the people "robust". They present no indication of what is called "rude" health. They are spare, and generally – so far as I can judge – rather undersized. At the same time their appearance cannot rightly by called sickly. Their movements are quick and easy, with nothing at all of languor expressed either in face or limbs. The hue of the skin is the least favourable characteristic. It is a tallowy-yellow. The faces which surround you in a factory are, for the most part, lively in character, but cadaverous and overspread by a sort of unpleasant greasy pallor. Now and then you observe a girl with some indication of roses in her cheeks, but these cases are clearly the exceptions to the rule; and amid the elder and matronly women not a single exceptional case of the kind did I observe. Altogether, the conclusion which a very careful examination of the physical appearance of the people led me to was this, that the labour cannot be said to exercise a seriously stunting or withering effect upon those subjected to it – that it does not, perhaps, make them actually ill, but that it does prevent the full development of form, and that it does keep under the highest development of health. Men and women appeared to be more or less in a negative sanitary condition. At any rate, what is called the "bloom of health" is a flower requiring more air and sunshine than stirs and gleams athwart the rattling spindle.

While we are making these observations,. however, the dinner-hour approaches. In Manchester everybody, master and man, dines at one o'clock. As the chimes sound, all the engines pause together, and from every workshop, from every industrial establishment – be it cotton, silk, iron, print works or dye works – the hungry crowd swarms out, and streets and lanes, five minutes before lonely and deserted, are echoing the trampling of hundreds of busy feet. The Manchester operative in prosperous times needs never want and seldom does want, a dinner of what he calls "flesh meat". This he sometimes partakes of at home, sometimes at a neighbouring cookshop; occasionally he has it brought to him at the mill. A favourite dish with the operatives is what they call potato pie – a savoury pasty made of meat and potatoes, well seasoned with pepper and salt, and roofed in with a substantial paste. Many of the men, after despatching their dinner, which they do comfortably in half an hour, spend the other moiety of their leisure in smoking or lounging about, until the never-failing bell proclaims that time is up, and that the engine and its attendant mechanism are ready to resume their labours. The work then proceeds until half after five o'clock, at which hour all labour finally ceases; the periods of toil having been from six o'clock until half past eight o'clock, from nine o'clock until one o'clock, and from two o'clock until half past five o'clock, making an aggregate of ten hours.[1] This arrangement, however, although very general, is by no means universal. Some of the mills do not open until seven o'clock, while a few prefer commencing at eight o'clock, after their people have breakfasted, and making but one stoppage during the day. There seems, however, to be a general, and I think a very well-founded opinion, that the division of the ten hours is a bad one inasmuch as it protracts the

[1] It is interesting to compare these hours with those operating 25 years earlier. *Sketch of the Hours of Labour, Meal Times, etc., in Manchester*, published in 1825, summarised the results of a survey made in the previous year. The mills were said to work on average a 14-hour day. Some did not stop for breakfast and by no means all the workers had an hour for dinner.

time of working until late in the evening, and casts the additional leisure, which it was the object of the Ten Hours Bill to secure to the workpeople, into the middle of the day, when they cannot well be expected to settle down to those domestic pursuits and means of self-improvement, which I am assured they are most eager to seize and avail themselves of, when they have a reasonable space to come and go upon between the closing of the mills and bedtime.

I stood to-day at the principal door of Messrs. Birley's establishment, watching the hands take their departure. It was curious to observe how each sex and age clung together. Boys kept with boys, men with men, and the girls went gossiping and laughing by, in exclusive parties of their own. I chanced to overhear a proposition confidentially made by one of these young ladies as she passed me to a comrade. There was not much in it, to be sure; but the proposal, at all events, showed that the fatigues of the day had by no means the effect of preventing a personal brushing-up for the evening. "I say, Jane," said the damsel in question, "I tell you what – you come home and braid my hair, and then I'll braid yours." The out-door dress of the men is comfortable and respectable. Velveteen jackets and shooting coats seem to be in great favour, with waistcoats and trowsers of dark fustian cloth. The people are uniformly well shod and their general appearance is that of unostentatious comfort.

I have taken some pains to ascertain in what way the mill operatives conduct the purchase of the tea and sugar which form so large a portion of their nourishment. I find that these are very generally purchased in pennyworths at small chandlers' shops. The customers commonly buy on credit, paying on the

Saturday night for what they have had during the previous week; but frequently require longer trust. They are always very particular in having a good pennyworth – that is, in having the draught of the scale in their favour; so that, with the credit demanded and the risk run, the profits of the vendor would be small indeed, were it not that he usually sells at 6s. a lb tea which the regular dealers sell at 4s. a lb. Thus the poor mill operatives pay higher by 33 per cent for their tea than their masters. In order to get rid of this disadvantage, the Messrs. Morris have started a co-operative society in their Chorlton mill. The mill is mapped out into twelve districts, the overlooker of each of which is furnished with a slip of paper, properly ruled and headed, in which each operative enters the amount of tea, at 5s. or 4s., black, green, or mixed; the amount of coffee, at 1s. 4d., 1s. 8d., and 2s.; that of cocoa at 8d. and 1s.; and that of chicory, which he or she may require during the week. The quantities of tea are reckoned in quarter pounds, those of coffee in half pounds. The different papers being filled up are carried to the Secretary of the Association, who casts up the sum total, and the people having paid for their week's supply when they received their wages, the amount, together with the order for the next week's consumption, is sent to a large wholesale house, which of course supplies a good article at wholesale price – that is to say, deducting half-a-crown in every pound of the nominal rate. Thus the average weekly supply costs about £20, and it is received for about £17 10s. The saving to the hands effected by this rate of discount, since the institution of the association three years ago, is calculated at £251 11s. 11d., and the saving from the 28th March to the 7th November of the present year has been no less than £69 7s. 1d. The collectors throughout the mill levy twopence on every pound subscribed, and out of this fund they make good to the wholesale house the deficiencies of any defaulter.

Similar systems, upon a larger scale, and embracing all sorts of provisions, have been tried, but found not to answer. "Not", says Mr. David Morris, "from any defect in the system itself, but because the workpeople mistook its object, tried to become dealers in the goods and to keep stocks on hand." The Tea and Coffee Association works admirably. At its starting, Mr. David Morris became responsible to the grocery house for the goods delivered, but that establishment is now quite content to give the operatives themselves credit, without any such collateral security.

I cannot quit the Messrs. Morris's establishment without mentioning the exertions which they have made for the ventilation of their mills, particularly in the card-room department. I saw one elderly woman who said that under the old system she was so asthmatic that she used every week to lay by a shilling to buy a bottle of physic to enable her to breathe. Since the ventilators have been at work she has never taken one drop of her medicine, and actually keeps the last phial, half full, as a trophy!

There are very various opinions afloat as to the extent of female immorality in the mills. It is the sincere conviction of a millowner in a town about thirty miles to the north of Manchester – a gentleman who has devoted a great deal of attention to the study of the social state of the cotton operatives – that there is hardly such a thing as a chaste factory girl, at least in the large towns. But this is an assertion the correctness of which is generally, and I believe with truth, denied.

The fact is, as I am assured, that there exists among the mill girls a considerable degree of correct feeling – sometimes, indeed, carried to the extent of a species of saucy prudery – upon these subjects. They keep up a tolerably strict watch upon each other, and a case of frailty is a grand subject for scandal throughout the whole community. Dr. Cooke Taylor narrates that, in a register of instances of seduction kept by a millowner, it was found that the guilty parties never belonged to the same factory. They met, not at work, but casually, and in other ways.[1] The number of bastardy warrants granted by the Manchester magistrates in 1848 was 53. Under these, two persons were discharged, eight summarily convicted, and 39 cases "amicably settled". There appears, however, to be no doubt whatever that prostitution is rare among the mill girls. In the Manchester Penitentiary, in 1847, the number of female inmates who had worked in mills amounted to only one-third of the number who had been domestic servants.

Speaking generally, the exceedingly quiet and inoffensive character of the Manchester mill population cannot be too highly esteemed. "After ten o'clock," says Sir Charles Shaw, the late head of the police, "the streets are as quiet as those of a country town." The statement may be a little, but not much, exaggerated.

In truth the Manchester operative is amongst the most industrious and patient of citizens. He toils cheerfully, and is day by day learning to read more, and to think more. If he has a turn for study, he devotes himself, in a few cases, to mechanical science – in the great number to botany. The science of plants is, indeed, a passion with the Manchester weaver. Every holiday

---

[1] W. Cooke Taylor, *Notes of a tour in the manufacturing districts of Lancashire*, London, 1842, p. 261.

sees hundreds of peaceful wanderers in the woods and fields around, busily engaged in culling specimens of grasses and flowers; while, generally harmless and industrious as the present generation are, there is good hope for expecting yet better things at the hands of their successors.

5. Calico Printing

IN INVESTIGATING the cotton trade and the condition of the cotton workers in Lancashire, I must not forget the important process of emblazoning the pure calico with those fantastic patterns which suit the taste of different purchasers in different markets. There is something curious, while walking through the stacks of coloured stuffs with which the rooms of a great warehouse are heaped, in the reflection that in the course of a year or so the piles of fabric which surround you will form the clothing and household drapery of half the nations of the east and south. This piece of gaily-tinted cloth will cover a divan in a Turkish harem – this other will flutter across the desert in the turban of an Arab sheik. Here is the raw material of a garment which will be stitched by Hindoo fingers – there a web which will be "made up" by a Chinese tailor; while beside it there may perchance be the staple of the flowing robe which the Tahiti girl will doff when she laves her limbs in the pellucid depths behind the coral reefs of the South Seas. As a general rule, the Mediterranean and Levantine nations prefer the most glaring patterns. The manufacturer can never make his reds, oranges, and yellows too bright for the taste of the Archipelago, the Smyrnioic cities, and the fashions prevalent among the African subjects of France.

"So you find a market in the military colony?" I said to a calico printer. "Yes," was the reply. "The French are an ingenious people. They go first and do the fighting, and we come quietly after them and sell our calicoes."

In what strange places do the circling waves of a diplomatic misunderstanding break! Possibly the only result of the difference between the Porte and the Czar will have been that it created a temporary slackness in the demand for calico, printed in staring colours and uncouth patterns, in the works round Manchester.

Calico printing, 1844

One of these situated upon the stream of the Medlock, before it descends to Manchester, I have recently visited. It is the calico-printing establishment of Messrs. Wood and Wright, and the great courtesy of the former gentleman I am pleased to have an opportunity of acknowledging. The process of calico-printing may be described as a modification of dyeing, combined with an adaptation of the process of letter-press machinery. The old block printing system, performed by hand, is becoming extinct. In the establishment of Messrs. Wood and Wright, at Bank-bridge, the block printers do not earn upon the average more than 8s. per week. Their wages when in full employment are much higher, but they are seldom in full employment. The lowest wages paid to adult men, working full hours, are 16s. per week. The machine printers make about 35s. a week, and the children employed in folding the stuffs, and in a variety of light duties, earn from 3s. 6d. to 5s. a week. There is one species of labour employing boys in the printing process, which certainly ought to be performed by machinery, and which is, without doubt, the most wearying and irksome which I have seen in Lancashire. It consists simply in turning a wheel, which causes cylinders to revolve in a dye-pit beneath. Here is a species of labour at once degrading, stupefying, and exhausting. It is paid for at the rate of 5s. a week, of twelve hours' daily toil.[1] The boys, as might be expected, plied their tasks lazily and listlessly. The superintendent of the department said that they were brisk and active, and merry enough, when released in the evening. It may be so, but I am bound to state that these boys were the only species of labourers whose condition I pitied since my arrival in Lancashire. The calico-printing process involves, in certain rooms, a necessity for a very high temperature, and a moist atmosphere, necessarily more or less impregnated with the fumes of chemical combinations. In one apartment in particular the steam of the boiling water gushed out in such profusion that the place seemed a mass of hot mist. The breathing was

---

[1] The Ten Hours' Act did not apply to calico printing works.

at first impeded, but in a second or so became free enough. The hand-block printing room was, however, the most unpleasant, and I should think the most injurious, not so much on account of the actual temperature or the fumes of the colouring matter, as by reason of the vast quantity of newly printed calico hanging up to dry, and completely stopping anything like a free circulation of the air. The bleaching and washing rooms were as healthful as may be – although the work must be rather a cold one in cold weather. Hot and steaming as are many of the processes, however, I could not ascertain that any evil sanitary consequences had been observedly developed. At least, the workpeople themselves said that they had no reason to complain; and of this I am certain, that a greater number of fat, jolly-looking personages than have been employed for years in Messrs. Wood and Wright's establishment I never saw. There is but a very insignificant proportion of women employed in calico print-works, and their duty chiefly consists in such coarse needlework as is required for stitching together the pieces.

6. Health

MANCHESTER occupies a bad pre-eminence in the statistics of death; and Manchester is the metropolis of cotton spinning; *ergo*, it has been a good deal the fashion to argue that death and cotton spinning go together. I have already described factory toil as a species of labour, light and easy of performance, seldom or never calling forth the full employment of all the energies, and allowing frequent periods of rest. The charges of over-crowding the people in factories arise from simple and sheer ignorance of what a factory is. In the most crowded department of a mill, the people cannot be placed nearly so closely as the passengers are in a first-class railway carriage, and for the simple reason that the vast proportion of each room is occupied by machinery. The ventilation and temperature of factories have next to be taken into consideration. As a general rule, I believe that the air which mill labourers breathe at their work is far better than the air which they breathe at home; and in this respect the condition of the mills is year by year improving. It is instructive, for example, to compare the amount of window-glass – in other words, the extent of the arrangements for admitting light and air – in the more recently built mills with those subsisting in the mills of older standing. The fact is, that the better the air, the better do the people work; and of this truth millowners are now fully aware. As a general rule, the worst ventilated mills being the old ones, are also provided with old machinery, and the obvious result is, that neither in amount nor quality of production can they compete with the newer mills. The owners of such establishments struggle under disadvantages so great as often to make them the first, at periods of depression, to go to wall. Within the last three weeks the price of raw cotton has considerably advanced, and two old-fashioned factories in Manchester have failed. In the mill-windows ample arrangements for swinging panes for admitting air are now almost universally made; and in by far the greater number of workrooms which I have visited, the air, if it did not smell wooingly, was at all events perfectly inoffensive. In certain mills – those spinning fine threads, or, as they are technically called, "high numbers" – an elevated temperature, say from 70 to 80, is required, and certainly kept up. In these rooms, attention to the ventilation is, of course, extremely requisite; but if this attention be, as it can be, duly enforced, the mere height of the temperature is not a matter of much sanitary consequence, except, perhaps, in relation to a certain forcing effect which it seems to exert on children, and also as regards the tendency it produces in the people to attempt to keep the thermometer up to a corresponding degree at their own homes.

The opinions of two medical gentlemen of Manchester, with whom I have conversed, come to this:– That the insalubrity of Manchester and of the Manchester operatives is occasioned, not by the labour of the mills, but by the defective domestic arrangements for cleanliness and ventilation. Each of the gentlemen in question has peculiar opportunities of observation. One of them, Mr Holland, surgeon, is one of the medical officers of the police and the poor-law authorities; the other, Dr Johns, is the registrar for one of the most populous operative districts of the town.

Before me lie several Reports, made to the Health of Towns Commission, on the sanitary state of the manufacturing districts. Little, if any, mention is made of the mills in these documents. But the reporters enter, with great minuteness of detail, into the home mode of living of the people, and deduce therefrom the cause of mortality.

Thus, Mr Holland, in his report on Chorlton-on-Medlock, proves that the mortality varies amongst the same class receiving the same wages in proportion as they inhabit second or third-class houses, and second or third-class streets. In first-class streets in Chorlton, the mortality is 1 in 46, a lower rate than the mortality of Brighton: in third-class streets it is 1 in 27, a higher rate than that of Liverpool. Again, in houses of the first class, the Chorlton mortality is 1 in 52, a proportion nearly as small as the mortality of Windsor; in the houses of the third class the mortality is 1 in 29, a proportion higher than that of the borough of Manchester.

A vast proportion of the mortality of Manchester is that of children, but of children, be it observed, under the age of labour in the mills. Out of every 100 deaths in Manchester, more than 48 take place under five years of age, and more than 51 under ten years of age. In some of the neighbouring towns – particularly Ashton under Lyne the proportion is still more appalling. There, by a calculation embracing the five years ended June 30, 1843, it appeared that, out of the whole number of deaths, 57 per cent. were those of children under five years of age.

It is, of course, generally known that the first five years of life are the most fatal in all districts; but upon comparing a series of cotton spinning districts in the North with a series of purely rural districts in the West and South, I find that, while the infant mortality in the former is about 50 per cent., speaking in round numbers, that of the latter is only about 33 per cent.

Manchester is a centre to which tramps and vagrants resort and to which immigrants flow from the agricultural districts, these last being very frequently in such bad health as to be incapable of longer pursuing field work. To such overflows all great capitals of industry will probably be ever more or less exposed, and such overflows will ever add to the due amount of sickness and death. But let there once exist a universal system of healthful sanitary regulation, and even the typhus generated by masses of poverty crowded together in search of work may be modified and kept under control. We have heard old legends of victims built up in thick walls of ancient donjon keeps cited as proofs of feudal tyranny. The day, let us be thankful, is dawning upon us when capitalists who run up ranges of streets, terraces and crescents, will be made aware that, in rearing cities without drains and water supplies, without light and air, they are committing crimes blacker than those of any old castellan – that they are sacrificing not one life, but scores of lives – that they are piling up fabrics of disease – building in with the very walls, masses of deadly typhus and cholera.

During the last few years the corporation of Manchester have been busy flinging open *culs-de-sac*, and running airy streets through overcrowded neighbourhoods. Parks are being provided with gymnastic apparatus for children; and an ample supply of the purest water is slowly but surely making its way from the distant hills.

7. Drugged Until They Die

THE UNDUE proportion of infant mortality arises from the neglect of mothers who are compelled to leave their young children at home while they labour in the mill. This I hold to be the blackest blot on the factory system. Whether it can be remedied is a question which I will not attempt to answer. "Pregnant women," says Dr Johns, "frequently continue their work up to the very last moment, and return to it as soon as ever they can move about." "In Ashton under Lyne", says Dr Coulthard, "it is no unfrequent occurrence for mothers of the tenderest age to return to their work in the factories on the second or third week after confinement, and to leave their helpless offspring in the charge of mere girls or superannuated old women." The same authority mentions the case of a nurse "suckling three of these children," and so exhausted as to be "unable to walk across the room" while the children were "almost unable to move their hands and feet". The inevitable result of this system is the reckless and almost universal employment of narcotics. First, the child is drugged until it sleeps, and then too often it is drugged until it dies.

There is not a more thoroughly household word through the cotton spinning towns than "Godfrey". Indeed, just as the gin-loving race of London delight to call their favourite beverage by dozens of slangy affectionate titles, just as there is "Cream of the Valley", and "Regular Flare-up", and "Old Tom", so there is to be found in the druggists' shops in the lower districts here, "Baby's Mixture", "Mother's Quietness", "Child's Cordial", "Soothing Syrup", and so forth, every one of these lulling beverages being a sweetened preparation of laudanum.

Druggists were exceedingly shy of giving any information upon the practice of dosing infants; but it is one of such great interest and importance that I resolved, *coute qui coute*, to obtain a body of evidence upon the subject. With this view I have waited upon many medical men, examined a great many elderly factory hands, male and female, and called at no fewer than thirty-five druggists' shops.

The information given to me by medical men was general in its character, and may be summed up in the evidence elicited from Mr John Greg Harrison, one of the factory medical inspectors, and a gentleman carrying on a very large practice amongst the operative classes.

"The system of drugging children is exceedingly common and one of the prevailing causes of infant mortality. Mothers and nurses both administer narcotics;

the former, however, principally with the view to obtaining an undisturbed night's rest. The consequences produced are imbecility, caused by suffusion on the brain, and an extensive train of mesenteric and glandular diseases. The child sinks into a low torpid state, wastes away to a skeleton, except the stomach, which swells, producing what is known as pot-belly. If the children survive the treatment, they are often weakly and stunted for life. To this drugging system, and to defective nursing, its certain concomitant – not to any fatal effect inherent in factory labour – the great infant mortality in the cotton towns is to be ascribed."

From evidence given me by mill hands, I select the following cases, observing that they merely serve as samples of the ordinary stories told me by those who were sufficiently candid to speak out upon the subject.

An intelligent male operative in the Messrs. Morris's mill in Salford stated that he and his wife put out their first child to be nursed. The nurse gave the baby "sleeping stuff" and it died in nine weeks. The neighbours told his wife how the baby was dosed, but the nurse denied that the child had ever got anything of the kind. They never sent a child out to be nursed again. For that one they paid 3s. 6d. a week, and the weeks that the nurse washed for it, 4s. The mother had to get up at four o'clock and carry it to the nurse's every morning; but the distance was too far for her to suckle it at noon, so the child had no milk until the nurse brought it home at night. The nurses are often old women, who take in washing, and sometimes they have three or four children to take care of. The mother can often smell laudanum in the child's breath when it comes home. As for mothers themselves, they give the "sleeping stuff" principally at night to secure their own rest.

"The poor child's nurse"

Another operative in the same mill gave the following evidence:– He had put out one child to nurse, and he and his missus had sorely rued it ever since. The child, a girl, had never been healthy or strong, and the doctors told them, when she was 14 months old, that she had been dosed, and how it would be with her. They paid 5s. a week to the nurse. His wife then earned 15s. a week in a mill. At present he thought that 4s. was about the average paid for nursing children. The nurses very often take in washing and put the infants to sleep by drugging them. He had six children, and they were all hearty except the first.

A female weaver in a mill at Chorlton stated the case of a little girl who was nursed by a neighbour of hers and who got "sleeping stuff". The child seemed to be always asleep and lay with its eyes half open. Its head got terribly big and its fingernails blue. The mother took the child from the nurse and carried it to the doctor, who said it was poisoned. The mother went on her knees crying, and said she had never given the child anything; but it died very soon after. The witness was a married woman, but had never had any family. She had often heard tell of the effects of "sleeping stuff" and how it killed the poor children.

Another woman, employed in the weaving room of the same mill, had put out all her children to nurse and had lost none of them. But she had a good kind nurse, a married woman, not one of the regular old nurses who made a trade of it. She had often heard of children getting "sleeping stuff". It made them that they were always dozing, and never cared for food. They pined away, their heads got big, and they died. She carried her own child every morning to the nurse, rising for this purpose a full hour before she went to the mill because the nurse lived some way off. The nurse did not rise at the same time, but she (the mother) put the baby into bed to her and left it there till the evening. She did not suckle it in the course of the day because the distance was too far to go. All her children were thriving.

I now come to the druggists. With one or two honourable exceptions, these individuals either point blank denied that the drugging system existed, or declined giving any information whatever. More than one of the proprietors of the most noted "Godfrey shops" in Manchester were amongst the latter class, while of the others, who repudiated the traffic entirely, several of them had their windows crowded with announcements of different forms of the medicine which they were cool enough to declare they did not deal in.

My inquiries extended to the use of laudanum in different forms by people of all ages, and I transcribe the evidence of those druggists from whom I received any information worthy of the name.

A highly-respectable druggist in Salford states as follows:– The use of laudanum as a stimulant by male and female adults is not at all uncommon. His sales in that way are, however, small. He disposes of about a shilling's worth weekly, in pennyworths. Some of his customers will take a tea-spoonful or a tea-spoonful and a half of laudanum; and in bad times, when they have no money, they come and beg for a dose. The sale of crude opium has, he thinks, diminished in his part of the town. When people come for laudanum, to use it as a stimulant, he sells it mixed with tincture of gentian, in the hope that it may do them less harm. Children are drugged either with Godfrey's Cordial or stronger decoctions of opium. Every druggist makes his own Godfrey, and the stronger he makes it, the faster it is bought. The medicine consists of laudanum sweetened by a syrup and further flavoured by some essential oil of spice. Mothers sometimes dose their infants, but the nurses carry the practice to the greatest extent. The mother takes the infant from the warm bed at five o'clock in the morning and carries it to the nurse's, where it is left till noon and often drugged to keep it quiet.

Among the druggists who were obviously disingenuous upon the point, I may particularly mention one, not far from the Rochdale-road. He tried to pooh-pooh the whole thing. "He sold nothing of the kind, at least next to nothing, nothing worth mentioning. Oh, no. The fact was that a great deal of nonsense was talked upon the subject. Isolated cases might be found, but to say there was anything like a general practice of drugging children was to raise a mere bugbear." Now, during our conversation, which occupied about five minutes, my cool and candid friend actually suited the action to the word by handing over the counter, to two little girls, three distinct pennyworths of the very drug the demand for which he was resolutely denying! I would have given something for that gentleman's power of face. I think it could be made useful.

Another druggist told me of a common feature in this hocusing system. The women go to shops where the "cordial" is made weak, and where a certain quantity, say half a teaspoonful, is prescribed as a dose. Afterwards they go to shops where the mixture is made stronger, and without making any further inquiry buy the drug and give the child the old dose. Yet some of the druggists, said this gentleman, "put twice or thrice as much laudanum into their Godfrey as others."

By a druggist carrying on an extensive business in a low neighbourhood in Ancoats, inhabited almost exclusively by a mill population, I was informed that personally he did not sell much narcotic medicine, but that it was tolerably extensively vended in small "general shops", the owners of which bought the drug by gallons from certain establishments which he named. He informed me also that he was in the habit of making Godfrey without putting laudanum into it, a system, from all I hear, very much akin to making grog without spirits. He affirmed, however, that the carminative ingredients, used for flatulence, constituted an important element of the medicine, and one for which it was frequently bought. He expressed his belief that the drugging system was gradually going out, and that the "old women" and midwives, who were its great patrons, were losing their hold upon the mill population. Recipes, which had been handed down in families for generations, and which often contained dangerous quantities of laudanum, were occasionally brought to him to make up, but he found little difficulty in convincing their possessors of the noxious character of the ingredients, when he was sometimes allowed to change their proportions. Sometimes a half-emptied bottle of cordial would be brought, in order that more laudanum might be put into it – a request which he always met by pretending to comply with it, and sending the applicant away with the contents of the phial increased by a few drops of harmless tincture. The mortality among infants in Manchester this gentleman attributed not to narcotics, but to careless nursing and insufficient and unwholesome suckling. "When women work nearly all day in a hot and close temperature, and live for the most part upon slops, their milk does children more harm than good. Infants are suckled hastily at dinner time, while the mother is eating her own meal, and then they are left foodless until well on in the evening. The consequence is a train of stomach complaints, which carries them off like pestilence. Children who had been drugged with 'sleeping stuff' he could recognize in a moment. They never appeared fairly awake. Their whole system appeared to be sunk into a stagnant state." He believed that when such doses were administered, nurses were chiefly to blame; for mothers often came to him with their ailing children, asking, in great trouble, whether he thought that "sleeping stuff" had anything to do with the child's illness. The proportion of illegitimate children carried off through inefficient nursing was terrible. As to adults, he knew that a good deal of opium and laudanum was taken by them. Women were his chief customers in that way. He had seen a girl drink off an ounce-and-a-half of laudanum as it was handed to her over the counter. Most of these people had begun by taking laudanum under medical advice and had continued the practice until it became habitual.

While we were talking, another druggist entered the shop and confirmed the main points of the above statement. He added that when he was an apprentice, twenty years ago, in a country place, principally inhabited by hand-loom weavers, his master used to make Godfrey in a large boiler by twenties and thirties of gallons at a brew. He believed that the people did not drug their children half so much now-a-days. Coroners' inquests were good checks. Almost all the laudanum he sold was disposed of in pennyworths. "A great number of old women took it for rheumatism."

I beg, however, to direct particular attention to the following evidence, given by a most intelligent druggist carrying on a very large business in a poor neighbourhood surrounded by mills, and a gentleman of whose perfect candour and good faith I have certain knowledge:–

"Laudanum, in various forms, is used to some extent by the adult population, male and female, and to a terrible extent for very young children. I sell about 2s. worth a week of laudanum, in pennyworths, for adults. Some use raw opium instead. They either chew it or make it into pills and swallow it. The country people use laudanum as a stimulant, as well as the town people. On market days, they come in from Lymm and Warrington, and buy the pure drug for themselves, and 'Godfrey' or 'Quietness' for the children. Habitual drunkards often give up spirits and take to laudanum as being cheaper and more intensely stimulating. Another class of customers are middle-aged prostitutes. They take it when they get low and melancholy. Three of them came together into my shop last night for opium to relieve pains in their limbs. These women swallow the drug in great quantities. As regards children, they are commonly dosed either with 'Godfrey' or 'Infant's Quietness.' The first is an old fashioned preparation and has been more or less in vogue for near a century. It is made differently by different vendors, but generally speaking it contains an ounce and a half of pure laudanum to the quart. The dose is from half a teaspoonful to two teaspoonfuls. Infant's Cordial, or Mixture, is stronger, containing on the average two ounces of laudanum to a quart. Occasionally paregoric, which is one-fourth part as strong as laudanum, is used. Mothers sometimes give narcotics to their children, but most commonly the nurses are at fault. The stuff is frequently administered by the latter without the mothers' knowledge, but it is occasionally given by the mothers without the fathers' knowledge. I believe that women frequently drug their children through pure ignorance of the effect of the practice, and because, having been brought up in the mills, they know nothing about the first duties of mothers. The nurses sometimes take children for 1s. 6d. a week. They are very often laundresses. Half-a-crown a week may be the average charge of the nurse, and the 'nursing' commonly consists of laying the infant in a cradle to doze all day in a stupefied state produced by a teaspoonful of 'Godfrey' or 'Quietness.' Bad as the practice is, it would not be so fatal if the nurses and parents would obey the druggists' instructions in administering the medicine. But this is what often takes place. A woman comes and buys pennorths of 'Godfrey'.

Well, all is right for five or six weeks. Then she begins to complain that we don't make the 'Godfrey' so good as we used to do; that she has to give the child more than it needed at first; and so nothing will do but she must have 'Infant's Quietness' instead, for, as she says, she has heard that it is better, i.e. stronger. But in process of time, as the child gets accustomed to the drug, the dose must be made stronger still. Then the nurses, and sometimes the mothers, take to making the stuff themselves. They buy pennorths of aniseed, and treacle and sugar, add the laudanum to it, and make the dose as strong as they like. The midwives teach them how to brew it, and if the quantity of laudanum comes expensive, they use crude opium instead. Of course numberless children are carried off in this way. I know a child that has been so treated at once; it looks like a little old man or woman. I can tell one in an instant. Often and often a mother comes here with a child that has been out to nurse, to know what can be the matter with it. I know, but frequently I dare hardly tell, for if I say what I am sure of, the mother will go to the nurse and charge her with sickening the child; the nurse will deny, point blank, that she did anything of the sort, and will come and make a disturbance here, daring me to prove what of course I can't prove legally, and abusing me for taking away her character. The children also suffer from the period which elapses between the times of their being sucked. The mothers often live on vegetables and drink quantities of thin ale, and the consequence is that the children are terribly subject to weakening attacks of diarrhoea."

Hearing in several quarters of the "little shops" which retailed "Godfrey", I looked out for such an establishment, and in a back street in Chorlton, surrounded by mills, I hit upon what I wanted, a shop in the "general line", in the window of which, amongst eggs, candies, sugar, bread, soap, butter, starch, herrings and cheese, I observed a placard marked "Children's Draughts, a penny each". There was a woman behind the counter, and on my making inquiries as to whether she sold "Godfrey" or any similar compound, she replied she had not for six months. The draught announced in the window was purgative.

"Then you used to sell 'Godfrey'?"

"Oh yes. We used to make it and sell it for children when they were cross; but people did not think ours strong enough."

"What did you make it of?"

"We took a pennorth of aniseed, a quarter of a pound of treacle, and a pennorth of laudanum (a quarter of an ounce). Then we stewed down the aniseed with water, and mixed up the whole in a quart bottle."

"And so this stuff was too weak?"

"Aye, that it was. I could have sold it fast enough if I had made it stronger; but I daren't do it for fear of getting into trouble."

"Do you ever give it to your own children?" – there were several sprawling about the back parlour.

"Yes. But I never put a pennorth of laudanum into the bottle that I gave it to them out of."

"But very strong stuff is generally used?"

"Indeed it is. You may know the children that get it at once – if you have any experience in them things – they're so sickly, and puny, and ill-looking. It's a shocking thing that poor people should be obliged to give their children such stuff to keep them quiet."

When we take into consideration this horrible system of juvenile "hocusing", this feeding infants upon loathsome syrupy laudanum rather than their mother's milk, when we duly ponder on the state of filth in which children left inefficiently attended must live (and the nature of the superintendence they receive is well illustrated by the fact that more than 4,000 go annually astray and get "lost" in the streets of Manchester) – and, finally, when we take into consideration such facts as those stated by the registrar of Deansgate, in Manchester, when he tells us that, in one district, nearly 200 children died in a year "without any reasonable attempt having been made to save them" – the miserable little wretches having been soothed and stupefied in their sickness by opiates – when we endeavour to realise in our minds in its full horror this foul and unnatural state of things, can we feel either shocked or surprised at the deliberate declaration of the registrar, that, in Manchester, in the course of seven years, there perished 13,362 children "over and above the mortality natural to mankind?" Yes: 13,362 "little children brought up in dwellings and impure streets – left alone long days by their mothers – to breathe the subtle sickly vapours – soothed by opium, a more cursed distillation than hebenon – and when assailed by mortal disease, their stomachs torn, their bodies convulsed, their brains bewildered, left to die without medical aid, which, like hope, should come to all, the skilled medical man never being called in, or only summoned to witness the death and sanction the funeral!"

There are two exciting causes for this mass of infantine misery. First, but in a comparatively small degree, the unhealthy state of the houses; secondly and mainly, the neglect and all the concomitant evils consequent upon the mothers of children of tender age passing their days in the mill. Herein – I cannot too often repeat it – lie, in my solemn conviction, the bane and disgrace of the cotton system.

8. The Quest for Knowledge

I HAVE already, in general terms, noticed the almost universal testimony borne by those who know the Manchester "mill hand" best, to the mild and inoffensive character and bearing of the cotton population. The colliers and metal workers throughout the north, indeed, profess to hold the men of the loom and the mule in great contempt, as a set of spiritless milksops – as soft and pliable as the fibre which they twist. And truly there can be little doubt but that the men who habitually deal with bobbins and threads must form a very different race to the sturdier and more turbulent spirits whose lot is cast among sledge-hammers and pick-axes. A turn-out of the cotton workers is a very different, and, generally speaking, a far less riotous affair than a strike in the districts of iron and coal.

As a general rule, the men of cotton are essentially a peaceful and moral force generation. They are greatly under the influence of leaders, whose mental powers they respect. There are not a few of the weavers and spinners whose capacity for thought is considerable; and these again have to deal with a population whose faith is one of their most distinguishing moral attributes. The cotton mills of Manchester abound with hard-headed, studious, thoughtful men, who pass brooding, meditating lives, sometimes taken up in endeavours to sound those profound social problems which lie at the bottom of the relations between capital and labour;

sometimes, again, occupied with the various phases of physical and mechanical science; and not unfrequently sturdy theologians, profoundly versed in the subtleties and casuistries of all the warring schools of Calvinism. In this respect, indeed, the Lancashire temperament is not unfrequently akin to that which so plentifully prevails to the north of the border. I have conversed with many operatives of the class which I have sketched, and generally left them with a very considerable respect for their self-acquired attainments, and their earnest if not enthusiastic tone of character. Such men often rise to be overlookers in their respective mills, and in many instances pass their evenings in teaching adult classes of their fellow labourers. As a general rule, they are nearly all either professed or virtual teetotallers, and as such are greatly given to the cant of temperance which denounces as a folly and a crime the most harmless degree of social indulgence. I had one long conversation with a man who was a good specimen of the class in question. He is now an overlooker in a mill in Hulme. He told me he had been a thoughtless scamp in his youth, and that he had led a vagrant sort of life, thinking of nothing but sensual pleasures until he became a man. Then he began to reflect upon the degrading life which he was leading, and to ask himself what was the use of his having a soul if he did not strive to elevate it; so, setting to work, he found – in his own words – that he was "endowed by God with a great capacity for study". He liked mechanical science the best, and now it was a great pleasure to him to strive to make his children fond of reading, and to educate and enlighten his fellow workmen. He was at the head of a small library, principally scientific. "Did they admit novels?" "Yes," with a melancholy shake of the head, "they found that they could not get on without something of that kind – the people liked stories." My friend, however, did not seem by any means "up" in the fiction department of his library, for he mentioned the "Pickwick Papers and other works by Eugene Sue". He highly approved of the cheap summer trips which the railways were giving the people. He had thus been able to "take his good woman one hundred and twelve miles from Manchester," and explained the country to her as they went along. Sometimes, in the department of which he was overlooker, they worked so fast that they got ahead of the others and had half a holiday. They were lucky in this respect lately. It was a fine day, and he had taken not only his own family, but all the workers in his department, out in a body to enjoy themselves in the fields, "a far better place than the public house."

Another intelligent operative I encountered in his own house, just as he returned from work. The room was cheery and clean. Two little girls with fat dimpled legs and arms sat on a stool before the fire. The plates and pot lids shone as brightly as old china or armour from the white-washed walls. The wife bustled with the tea things, and the good man sat him down in his rocking chair – that delicious piece of furniture of which the Yankees borrowed the idea from Lancashire and now impudently take credit for having invented.

My friend was a Ten Hours Bill man: "The people had health, and time, and spirits now to clean their houses and teach themselves something useful. The cotton folks were improving. Oh, yes, they were; and the next generation would be better than the present. No one ever thought of schools for children when he was a child. No; he had wrought many and many a time for twelve hours a day when he was not eight years old. The children were lucky now to what they were in them old times. There were good evening classes too for the men and women, only he was afeard that a good many of them, particularly the boys and girls, were too fond of going to the music saloons, where they did not hear no good, and did not do no good. He had gone to one himself lately". A look from his wife. "Oh, of course only to hear what was going on – only that – and he was disgusted, he was. Nigger songs," and with a significant wink, "other songs, and nonsensical recitations and trash – and girls dancing on the stage with such short petticoats. Oh, places like them wasn't no good. But there was the Monday night concerts – *there* was music – there was the place for a working man to have a rational night's amusement."[1]

In prosecuting my Ten Hours Bill inquiries, I picked up a good deal of information respecting the evening pursuits of the rising generation. Girls and young men, by the score and the hundred, appear to be learning to read, write, cipher and sew. Some had friends in America, and they wanted to send them the news. Others were the oldest in the family, and it behoved them to set their little brothers and sisters a good example. The girls made their own clothes, too "clothes of all sorts – paletots and visites, and they were very fond of sampler work". I have seen a great many of these samplers. In nine cases out of ten they commemorate the death of a relation – very often of a brother. They exhibit a tombstone and a weeping willow, with a verse of poetry or a sentence from the Bible beneath. The poetry was commonly of the 'afflictions sore long time I bore' school favoured by the

---

[1] See page 104.

national churchyard muse. They copied it, they said, from books or from old samplers, but sometimes they composed it themselves. No young lady would, however, plead guilty to any of the elegaic effusions which were exhibited. The men had frequently learned to write since they were grown up. They were anxious to read well also that they might avail themselves of the libraries. The lads were in a great proportion of cases members of night schools. One stout young fellow whom I asked if he was learning to read, replied, "No, he professed – the fiddle," and presently introduced a couple of youths who professed the fiddle likewise. Their musical preponderating over their literary tastes, the trio had clubbed together to engage the services of a master, and having got over the preliminary difficulties, they now met every night to practise and improve.

I have visited a great many children's schools – factory and mixed schools, and the first and last thing which struck me was that the children were decidedly smarter looking and more intelligent than the non-labouring juveniles. "They're not backward, sir," said the excellent and intelligent master of the Lyceum in Great Ancoats-street, "especially at mischief." In the All Saints National School, Chorlton, there were no factory children. The master described the boys as being principally the sons of small tradesmen and artisans. They appeared unintelligent, noisy, and indifferent. The master spoke despondingly of the prospects of education in Manchester. The system he thought was too slight and superficial to produce much practical effect. There was, of course, a degree of anxiety on the part of parents that their children should be educated, or his "scholars would not be there." The teacher appeared intelligent and conscientious, but he had evidently small faith in his prospects of success.

Cotton mills and canal, Union Street, 1829

From his school I went straight to another, entirely a factory one, and situated in the most densely-peopled part of operative Manchester. The Lyceum is close to Union-street, and Union-street is a locality which merits a word or two of special description. As Lancashire is to England; and as Manchester is to Lancashire, so is Union-street to Manchester. The locality is the very incarnation of the spirit of the district. A more perfectly ugly spot you shall not find between sunrise and sunset. Fancy a street one side of which is all mills, huge square piles of mills, with six, seven and eight tiers of foul and blackened windows, the grimiest, sootiest, filthiest lumps of masonry in all Manchester. Through the thick, sunless air comes the throb and the boom of many steam engines, and the clattering whirl of hundreds of thousands of revolving pirns and bobbins. Look in at the lower ranges of filth-encrusted windows. What multiplying revelations of endless carding frames, and drawing frames and tenting frames. Above, ponderous masses of hammered iron, the limbs of toiling engines, appear ever and anon to rush to the open window, glance abroad, and then retreat to their dens. On the other hand lies a canal – the Rochdale Canal – a ditch of muddy water, very much like rotten pea soup. Curious, old-fashioned, highly-springing bridges span it. On the further side are tumble-down houses, smouldering edifices, sinking into their foundations of muck and mire – filthy wharfs, littered with dung, and bricks, and rubbish heaps of splintered stones lie along its course. Blacksmiths' forges are established in rickety old tenements, with every pane of glass in their casements long since dashed away. Mean streets, and patches of black waste ground, with mouldering fences and fetid pools back these wharfs and ruinous forges; and a dingy fringe of second-rate mills, with puffing steam gushes and everlasting volumes of smoke, shut in the cheerless picture.

Close to this dreary but characteristic street are the Lyceum Factory Schools. The establishment boasts of a News-room and a Library. In the former, a quiet comfortable room, a fair assortment of the London and local journals are taken. The library is one of three thousand volumes. In the day-time, the children from the neighbouring mills receive their three hours' modicum of instruction; at night, adult classes meet in the same rooms. The children are charged three pence and fourpence a week, according as they remain half the day or the whole day in the school. Adults pay two shillings a quarter for classes, library, reading-room and all. The afternoon studies were proceeding when I entered the noisy room. Before me, ranged with their slates upon benches, or standing round chalked rings on the floor, were some three score of the little carders and scavengers from the dreary mills of Union-street. A set of more animated dirty faces and brighter, twinkling eyes you would find nowhere. The little fellows were tolerably ragged, to be sure – and some of them shoeless – but full of life, fun and devilry. One class was copying, upon their frameless slates, the word 'Britannia' chalked upon a large blackboard. I asked them what was the meaning of Britannia. They looked at each other, shuffled their feet – half a dozen were about to speak, when one urchin roared out, "Britannia? Why, to be sure, 'Britannia rules the waves'." And there was a great laugh at the appositeness of the quotation. Another class were spelling, under the care of an "apprentice teacher", a singularly fine-looking and intelligent boy. The pupils spelt very fairly a variety of dissyllabic and trisyllabic words. A third class were reading a simple account of the discovery of America. The school was not so crowded as usual, because one of the steam engines in Union Street had broken down.

"And what has the steam engine to do with it?" I naturally asked.

"Everything," was the reply. "When an engine ceases here, everything ceases – there are no wages, no fees, no schools."

Each spinner is obliged by the Factory Act to pay for the education of his piecers and scavengers. The fees are sometimes collected in the mills, but occasionally the boy is entrusted with the amount himself, the consequences of which piece of faith are not unfrequently a day's truant-playing, and a terrific debauch on unripe apples, toffy and gingerbread. Mr.

Clay, the principal master of the Lyceum, informed me that he had great difficulty in instilling anything like a moral sense into the children – particularly as respects lying. They saw no moral degradation in the idea of a falsehood. It was only inconvenient to be found out. The boys, too, were obstinately dirty, and he had often to send them home to wash themselves. In summer they seldom wore shoes. Mr. Clay is confident that a vast deal is being effected for the factory population by the education now being provided for them.

"Do you lose sight of the children when they leave school?" I asked. The answer was cheering – "No, especially the girls, for they come back often to the library for books."

Mr. Clay teaches a night adult class. He has grey-haired scholars, and sometimes mothers bring their children. This class had "decidedly increased" since the Ten Hours Bill. The worthy teacher was anxious to impress upon me that the young men and women attending the evening schools were kept very carefully apart. "I sometimes tell the young women that they only come to pick up sweethearts; but I take care that the one set has gone before I dismiss the other."

The Manchester Mechanics' Institution is supported by decidedly a better class than the average of mill operatives – that is to say, by workmen exercising a more skilled species of labour, and by shopmen. In the pianoforte class there are thirty-five pupils, generally tradespeople's daughters. The library is a good one. The books principally inquired for are, first, novels and romances; secondly, voyages, travels and biographies;

thirdly, philosophic works. Books in foreign languages are rarely demanded.

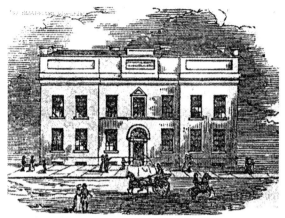

Manchester Mechanics Institute, Cooper Street

Every London publisher knows that Lancashire furnishes no unimportant part of the literary market of England. I was very desirous of ascertaining, therefore, the species of works most in demand amongst the labouring and poorer classes. The libraries in the better parts of the town are of course stocked in much the same way as the libraries in the better parts of London. I wished to ascertain the species of cheap literature most in vogue and I accordingly applied to Mr Abel Heywood, of Oldham-street, one of the most active and enterprising citizens of Manchester, who supplies not only the smaller booksellers of the town, but those throughout the county, with the cheap works most favoured by the poorer reading classes. The contents of Mr Heywood's shop are significant. Masses of penny novels and comic song and recitation books are jumbled with sectarian pamphlets and democratic essays. Educational books abound in every variety. Loads of cheap reprints of American authors, seldom or never heard of amid the upper reading classes here, are mingled with editions of the early Puritan divines. Double-columned translations from Sue, Dumas, Sand, Paul Feval and Frederic Soutie jostle with dream-books, scriptural commentaries, Pinnock's guides, and quantities of cheap music, Sacred Melodists and Little Warblers. Altogether the literary chaos is very significant of the restless and all-devouring literary appetite which it supplies. Infinitely chequered must be the *morale* of the population who devour with equal gusto dubious Memoirs of Lady Hamilton and authentic narratives of the "Third Appearance of John Wesley's Ghost", duly setting forth the opinions of that eminent shade upon the recent speeches of Dr Bunting.

So much for the *prima facie* aspect of Mr Heywood's literary warehouse. I was courteously furnished with details of his business, which throws an unquestionable light upon the tastes of the operative reading world of Lancashire.

That species of novel, adorned with woodcuts, and published in penny weekly numbers, claims the foremost place. The contents of these productions are, generally speaking, utterly beneath criticism. They form as far as I can judge, the English reflection, exaggerated in all its most objectionable features, of the French *Feuilleton Roman*. In these weekly instalments of trash, Mr Heywood is compelled to be a large dealer, as will appear from the following statement :

> Angelina
> Almira's Curse
> Claude Duval
> Eardley Hall

Ella the Outcast
Gentleman Jack
Gambler's Wife
Gallant Tom
Lady Hamilton
Mazeppa
Mildred
Old Sanctuary
Royal Twins
String of Pearls
The Brigand
The Oath

These average 6,000 weekly sale. All this mass of literary garbage is issued by Lloyd, of London, in penny numbers.

Of similar works, published also in numbers at 1d. per week, Mr Heywood sells :

Adam Bell	200
Claude Duval (Dipple)	400
Court of London	1500
Gretna Green	460
Love Match	750
Mysteries of London	1000
Nell Gwynne	700
Perkin Warbeck	100

Of the penny weekly journals, some of them, such as *Barker's People*, are political and democratic, but the greater number are social and instructive. The Lancashire sale is :

Barker's People	22000
Reynold's Miscellany	3700
Illustrated Family Journal	700
London Journal	9000

Family Herald	8000
Home Circle	1000
Home Journal	1000
Penny Sunday Times	1000
Lancashire Beacon	3000
Plain Speaker	200
Potter's Examiner	1500
Penny Punch	360
The Reasoner	160
Chat	200

Of these publications, the *Lancashire Beacon* and the *Reasoner* are avowedly infidel. I have not had an opportunity of seeing the latter, but in the number of the former which I perused, I found nothing more fatal to Christianity than abuse of the Bishop of Manchester. The Lancashire mind is indeed essentially a believing, perhaps an over believing one. Fanaticism rather than scepticism is the extreme into which it is most likely to hurry. In Ashton under Lyne, Johanna Southcote's bearded followers still meet under the roof of the New Jerusalem. In remote districts astrologers still watch the influences of the planets; and all quackeries, moral and physical – the remedies of Professor Mesmer or of Professor Holloway[1] – equally find a clear stage and very great favour.

---

[1] Franz Anton Mesmer (1734-1815) and Thomas Holloway (1800-1883). Mesmer, an Austrian mystic and physician, introduced Mesmerism (a forerunner of hypnotism), which was much in vogue during the 1840s. Holloway made a fortune from patent medicines, which were advertised on a scale previously unknown. Between 1845 and 1851, his advertising budget rose from £10,000 to £20,000 a year.

But to return to the cheap book trade of Lancashire. Of the better class of weekly publications, generally selling at 1½d., Mr Heywood makes the following return:

Domestic Journal	600
Eliza Cook's Journal	1250
Chambers' Journal	900
Chambers' Information for the People	1200
Hogg's Instructor	60
People's Journal	400

The cheap double-columned editions of Dickens' and Bulwer's works sell as follows :

Dickens	250
Bulwer	200

The sale of *Punch* is 1,200. *The Family Friend* sells 1,500 monthly at twopence; the *Family Economist* 5,000 monthly at one penny.

Mr Heywood informed me that the sale of cheap books has decidedly not increased in consequence of the Ten Hours Bill. The same assertion was made by another extensive though a much smaller bookseller in the vicinity of Garrett Lane. The department of the literary trade which alone seemed to have received any impetus from recent legislation was the sale of copy books. The only classification of the purchasers of cheap literature which I found it practicable to make was that the comic or *soi-disant* comic publications were usually patronised by clerks and shopmen, while tales were inquired for by the working classes, commonly so called. It is, indeed, by the links of a story that the operative taste seems to be most bound. For the encouragement of literary speculators, I may add that every cheap book is sure of a sale in Lancashire – at first.

At the library of the Mechanics' Institute, and at that of the Ancoats Lyceum, I was informed that the Ten Hours Bill made no change in the reading habits of the subscribers.

In educating the poor, the workhouses have unfortunately a great part to play – now more, now less, according to the pressure of the times. From the scholars who frequent either small private schools, often held in close, unventilated and incommodious rooms, and the scholars who resort to the larger and better seminaries, supported by, or in connexion with, the great Educational Association, and with local funds – from each and all of these scholars a weekly sum of pence is extracted. The fees of some schools are as low as 2d.; the terms of others, for the more advanced children, amount to 7d. But the pauper can neither have his two-pennyworth nor his seven-pennyworth of learning – those who feed and clothe must teach him, or he grows up a savage in his ignorance. When manufacturers have massed together vast populations so rapidly that the growth of the toiling crowd has far outstripped the decent and healthful accommodation which ought to be provided for it; and where, consequently, operative life is short, and sickness frequent and severe – in such social conditions the extent even of chronic pauperism must be considerable. But besides, the administrators of the Poor-law know well the perpetual crowd of hangers-on, which as it were floats round the skirts of northern industry – a crowd of nondescript composition, the supernumeraries of the cotton spinning cities – men and women who are content to live by a little labour and a good deal of charity – who pulsate backwards and forwards, as the shades of trade vary, between the workhouse and the mill. So, therefore, it happens that great hosts of children are always dependent upon the rate-payers for education as well as food. On the 1st of July, 1848, there lived in Manchester union 1,206 children under sixteen years of age; in the Salford union, 253; in the Chorlton union, 255. On the same day there lived in the town, as out-door paupers of the Manchester union, 7,048 children under sixteen years of age; as paupers of the Salford union 3,220; as paupers of the Chorlton union 1,603. This plain statement indicates at once the amount of juvenile pauper ignorance with which the Poor-law administration has to grapple – that of the children resident in the workhouse – and it indicates too, the far greater amount of juvenile ignorance over which the Poor-law administration can exercise little if any control – that of the outdoor pauper population. Making the proper deductions for children under a teachable age, it is the opinion of Mr. Browne, the Government inspector of parochial union schools for the North of England, that the number of out-door pauper children receiving "little or no education", is not under 100,000 – being ten times the number of the children in the workhouses.

This fact only requires to be plainly and broadly stated. Of course, the ignorance of these young English savages is dense and deplorable. The statement of the schoolmaster at the Canal-street Workhouse in Manchester, that only one in twelve of the children who came into that establishment could repeat the Lord's Prayer, proves the fact only in a very modified degree; for the reports of the school inspectors as to the frequency with which children can prate a form of words compared with the rarity of their understanding the meaning, warrant me in asserting that perhaps not one in twenty-four could give any intelligible account of the meaning of the prayer, or of the source from whence it came.

Workhouse boys

The children in workhouses throughout the manufacturing districts commonly attend school from nine to twelve o'clock in the forenoon and from two to half past four or five in the evening. In some workhouses the school-room is in the building. In others the children go to school beyond the union walls – sometimes to national schools, where "it is possible that the teachers do not always take the same pains with the young paupers" as with the other scholars – sometimes (I am still quoting Mr. Browne's Report for 1847-8) to schools "of a very inferior description, where the teachers are either negligent or incapable". As a general rule, Mr. Browne finds the children sent to school out of the workhouse "ignorant and ill instructed". But, indeed, the species of education generally afforded in the workhouse schools is very low and unsatisfactory. In twenty-five workhouses in Mr. Browne's district the teachers were paupers. Occasionally these men and women are neither precisely paupers nor independent persons. They live in the workhouses on the rates, but receive a small salary. Some of these teachers are, as might be expected, grossly incompetent – unable to write a decent hand or to spell an ordinary word. Those who have sunk into the workhouse from a good position, requiring fair educational attainments, are often morally unfit to be entrusted with the rearing of youth. In the Burnley workhouse, the teacher combined the duties of a porter with those of the school-room. The mistresses are frequently inefficient. One believed that Saul and Paul were identical; another described the miracles of Christ as having been wrought before Pharaoh. Neither of these persons is now a teacher. The position of a workhouse instructor is, however, described as being by no means an enviable one. It is a post of much confinement, of frequent collision with the union authorities, and generally of such a nature that no master who can procure a situation elsewhere will accept it. "The schools, therefore," continues Mr. Browne, "are likely to remain stationary when a certain point has been reached – by no means advanced – and below that where education may be expected to make a lasting impression upon the child, and consequently to operate as a check upon pauperism." But in many instances, ground has yet to be got over before even the lowest educational point worthy of the name is attained. For example, in Kirkham, an island was described as a "place where nobody lives". In Haslingden, none could say in what county they dwelt; and in Preston, by a most singular confusion of ideas, "prophecy" was defined as fortune-telling.

In a great many of the workhouse schools, however, education, though of a low species, is actually progressing, and the teachers, according to their capacity, strive to do their duty. The larger towns generally take the lead, and in these the inspector frequently found competent and intelligent masters and gradually improving pupils. In many instances the remark is "inefficient, but promising", and teachers are often spoken of as earnest and painstaking. The two great cities of Lancashire support two great pauper educational establishments, which may in some respects be reckoned models. Manchester has its Swinton[1] and Liverpool its Kirkdale. In the infant school attached to the former establishment, the children could point to Washington and Iceland on the map. They named the books of the Testament, and understood what a thermometer was. In the girls' school, five sevenths of the pupils could read the New Testament. They were also taught to sew, knit, cut out, wash, iron and mangle. In the boys' school, the reading was "fair" and a "certain standard of education attained by many"; so that "material progress may be expected". The industrial training consisted of tailors' and shoemakers' work, and clogging, and the general discipline was "excellent." At the Kirkdale establishment, the boys' school was efficient; but the infant and girls' schools were less satisfactory, and the progress of the learners slow. The

---

[1] The Manchester Union Moral and Industrial Training School with accommodation for 1,500 children and staff was built by the Manchester Board of Guardians in 1843. *Household Words*, of July 13, 1850, called it "a pauper palace."

girls sew and do household work, being out of school one week in three.

I have endeavoured to collect together at least some portion of the facts which, in surveying the moral and educational condition of cotton-spinning Lancashire, come most naturally to the surface. I know that beneath that surface there lies dormant a terrible mass of unmoved stolid ignorance, and strongly developed animal passion and instinct; but from the machinery which is at work, from the ideas which are making way, I believe that that mass will be, sooner or later, shaken and probed to its inmost depths. Education is but yet opening its trenches and arranging its batteries. The social and sanitary pioneers, which must precede education, have but just begun in earnest to advance. I believe that we must have a comfortable and a cleanly living people before we have an educated or a moral people; and, odd as the conjunction may seem, I believe that neither church nor school will do what each is capable of doing until drains are dug, and men's homes are sweetened and purified, and rendered fit not only for the preservation of due physical health, but of due social decency and modest reserve.

9. Sunday Schools

THE SUNDAY schools of the industrial North form not only a vast moral and educational engine, but a curious and characteristic social fact. The system originated by Mr. Raikes some seventy years ago took deep root in Lancashire, and grew with the growth of manufacturing industry. The serious cast of the Lancashire mind, and its earnestness and zeal, acting upon the facilities afforded by the order and discipline which it is the very nature of the factory system to instil, formed a soil in which the Sunday school system took very deep root and bore very rich harvests. I rather understate than overstate the numbers when I say that in the Sunday schools of Manchester may be found from 40,000 to 50,000 scholars, and from 4,000 to 5,000 teachers, inspectors and visitants. In 1832, the fiftieth anniversary of the foundation of the system was celebrated by a day of jubilee, and upon that occasion no fewer than 32,000 medals were disposed of, to be worn by members of the Sunday scholars' procession which defiled through the streets of Manchester. "Were it not for the Sunday schools," I have been over and over again assured, "Lancashire would have been a hell upon earth." Long before educational committees of the Privy Council and British and Foreign Societies were heard of, long previous to the era of Institutes and Athenaeums, the Sunday schools were sedulously at work, impregnating the people with the rudiments of an education which, though always rude and often narrow and fanatical in its teachings, was yet preserving a glow of moral and religious sentiment, and keeping alive a degree of popular intelligence which otherwise would assuredly have perished in the rush and clatter with which a vast manufacturing population came surging up upon the land. The early patrons and early champions of Sunday schools are now dying fast away. The great world has never heard of them, but yet amongst a large and, influential class in the north they have left immortal memories. Often and often have I lately had occasion to see the walls both of drawing-rooms and humble kitchen parlours, hung with portraits of grave, sober-clad men, whose names I have never heard of, and who were yet pointed out to me as among the greatest and most glorious of Englishmen. Local poets, too, have hymned the departure of locally famous Sunday school worthies. To those who know nothing of the excellent men commemorated, there is something which almost savours of the ludicrous in such a couplet as:

> *"–Oh was it not*
> *The meek and earth unblazoned name of Stott."*

Yet Mr. Stott was a hero in his way. He was for half a century the foremost champion of the Lancashire Sunday schools. When he commenced his labours he had to struggle against all the chimera terrors with which the first French Revolution peopled England. If he assembled a knot of children on the Sunday afternoon, he was accused of preaching Jacobinism to the rising generation. If he caused the children to walk in orderly procession from the school-room to the church, he was drilling them in military tactics, preparatory to the outbreak of an operative *Jacquerie*. Yet Mr. Stott worked steadily on. He began with two score pupils. In the school which he founded, I last Sunday saw two thousand six hundred.[1] Sunday schools in Manchester form not only a great educational engine, but a great social fact. Nearly every school has its library, and besides the library, many have their sick and burial societies. At Whitsuntide, the yearly week of rest in Manchester, nearly every school enjoys its gala and its country trip. Many of the richest and most prosperous men in Manchester will tell you, that to the Sunday school, which taught them to read and write, and

---

[1] David Stott (1779-1848), founder in 1801 of the Bennett Street Sunday School. See George Milner, Bennett Street Memorials, Manchester, 1880, pp. 121-140.

inculcated honesty and sobriety, they now owe their villas and their mills. Sunday schools, as they are worked in Lancashire, more than any set of institutions which I know, tend to bind different classes of society to each other. Men in the middle ranks of life very commonly act as teachers, or at all events take a practical interest in the proceedings; and acquaintanceships first formed in the class-room, lead, in very many cases, to subsequent and often life-long business connections. It often happens that families are for generations connected, as pupils or teachers, with the same Sunday school. "A great number of the children before you," I have been repeatedly told, "are the children of old scholars, and a great many of our teachers were themselves scholars in the classes which they now instruct."

The education afforded in the Manchester Sunday schools is, of course, of an elementary and religious character. The pupils are first taught to read; then scriptural extracts or the Scriptures themselves are put into their hands, and instructions in psalmody are diversified by familiar moral and doctrinal addresses and examinations into the contents of the chapter or passage last studied. The general description applies pretty well to all the Sunday schools connected either with the Church or with Dissent. Most of the schools, however, meet upon week days and week evenings, when secular instruction is communicated, consisting principally of reading, writing, cyphering and a little geography. The Sunday education is purely gratuitous. For that which goes on upon working days a small fee, varying from 2d. to 6d. a week, is commonly charged. Many Sunday schools have adult classes for men and women. I have repeatedly seen grey-haired scholars. In general, the ages of the pupils vary from eight to twenty, the girls commonly remaining in connection with the school longer than the young men.

There are in Manchester, connected with the Church, about fifty Sunday schools. Upon Whit Saturday every year the pupils of most of these schools walk in procession through the streets; and turning to the files of the *Manchester Guardian*, I copy the names of the twelve schools which last year brought the largest number of pupils into the field. These are:-

St. Paul's, Bennett-street	2,600
St. Paul's, German-street	1,400
St. Stephen's	800
St. George's, Hulme	777
St. Simon's	580
St. John's	560
St. Michael's, Miller Street	550
The Cathedral School	500
St. Ann's	500
St. James's ...	500
All Saints	450
St. Mathias', Salford	400
Making a total of	9,617

The number of scholars attending the other schools ranges, with one or two exceptions, above 200 apiece, and the sum total may be taken, on a rough calculation, to be somewhere about 25,000.

Besides the Church schools, there are in the Manchester district two "unions," as they are called, or communities of dissenting Sunday schools, termed respectively the Manchester and the Salford Union.

I have before me various published returns relative to the Manchester union, but I am informed that their details are so incorrect that I can only venture upon giving general results. The religious denominations in connection with the union are six – Independents, Baptists, Wesleyan Association, Primitive Methodists, New Connexion, and Welsh Calvinists. The number of schools is 28, with a total of 9,658 scholars. The average morning attendance is 4,527; in the afternoon the average is 6,525. The libraries connected with these schools contain a total of 16,527 volumes, and almost every school has its sick and burial society.

The Salford union consists of schools in connection with the following religious bodies:-

Wesleyan Methodists, 1 school	783 pupils
Primitive Methodists, 1 school	293 pupils
Independents, 6 schools	3,167 pupils
Association Methodists, 3 schools	657 pupils
New Connexion Methodists, 1 school	246 pupils
Baptist	386 pupils
Total	5,532 pupils

Besides these, there are schools in connection with bodies of Welsh and Scottish Calvinists. The exact numbers taught by the Roman Catholic Sunday schools I have not been able exactly to come at, but there are six or seven chapels, each having numerously attended schools connected with them. The above rough data will, I think, prove that my general estimate of the number of children attending Sunday schools in Manchester does not overshoot the mark. And, I may add, that more than half of these children attend school during the week likewise. Before proceeding to give a more particular account of the schools which I visited, I would wish to state – as showing the extent to which the moral restraint exercised by these institutions goes – that when, on the famous 10th of April, a great Chartist meeting was being held, under circumstances of intense public excitement, within three minutes' walk of the largest establishment of the kind in Manchester, the number of pupils in attendance was only six beneath that of the previous day.[1] The school is that of St. Paul, Bennett Street, the one founded by Mr. Stott, and that to which taking it as a good example of the Church schools – I last Sunday paid a very lengthened visit.

The Bennett-street Sunday school is a vast plain building, fully as large as an ordinary sized cotton factory, and exhibiting four long ranges of lofty windows. The number of pupils at present on the books is 2,611, and the average attendance 2,152. The number of Sunday scholars who learn writing and arithmetic, two evenings a week, paying for their paper, pens and ink, &c., is 260. The number attending the daily schools and paying twopence per week is 350. The members of the School Funeral Society amount to 1,804, and of the School Sick Society to 400. The total amount of relief afforded by these societies since their commencement is upwards of £7,285. I may add that in one evening in each week the female scholars are instructed in plain sewing and housewifery.

I have said that the building is composed of four stories; the girls occupy the two highest, the boys the two lowest. As to ages, the former ranged from little

---

[1] April 10, 1848, was the day on which Chartists from all parts of the country presented a monster petition to Parliament. There had been widespread fears of an uprising in support of the reformers, but the event passed off peacefully.

things of five and six, brought by their elder sisters, to well-grown young women. Many of them were the children of small shopkeepers and mechanics, the others were mill hands. Every girl there was decently attired and many of them were neatly and tastefully dressed. They sat in classes, engaged, according to their progress, in reading Scripture or Scriptural extracts. One roomful was preparing to go to church and practising choral versions of the responses, easily and gracefully arranged. The girls, however, did not sing with anything like the spirit and effect which the boys beneath threw into a concluding hymn. Perhaps the chanting of the responses presented more difficulties than the more familiar rhythm of one of Dr. Watts's hymns. Descending to the most crowded of the boys' rooms, I found that all the classes had just concluded reading the chapter in St. John giving an account of the interview of Nicodemus with Christ, and that one of the teachers, installed in a reading desk, was questioning the scholars upon the chapter. As a general rule, the questions were answered intelligently and readily – the demand for a definition of the word "Pharisee" being the greatest stickler propounded. At the courteous invitation of Mr. George Lawton, the superintendent present, I selected a class to hear them read, pitching upon one composed of boys of medium age – say from 12 to 14. They read, without exception, fluently and correctly – the only marked feature in the performance being the inevitable pronunciation of the letter "U" in "up", for example, as if the word were spelled "oop". But this is a common peculiarity of teachers as well as scholars. Glancing around the class, which was composed in the main of commonplace-looking boys, dressed, some of them, in fustian, others in coarse cloth, and generally sallow-faced, thin and rather undersized, as Manchester urchins too often are – I thought I would like to know something about the social position of each, and accordingly, with the sanction of the master, examined the boys *seriatim*. The following are the results:-

1. Is ten years old. Works ten hours a day in the card-room, and makes 5s. 10d. a week, which he gives his parents. They allow him fourpence or sixpence for pocket money. Can read and write.

2. Is fifteen years of age. Is in a greengrocer's shop all day, for which he gets half-a-crown a week. Goes on week nights to the Lyceum school. Can write a little.

3. Is fourteen years of age. Works six hours and a half a day at a boiler-maker's. Only goes to the Sunday-school. Has 3s. a week. Gives it to his mother. Can write.

4. Is fourteen years of age. Also works in an engine-shop twelve hours a day for 3s. Can write, because he was taught at Sunday school.

5. Is thirteen years of age, and works in a machine-shop from six in the morning till eight and nine, and sometimes ten o'clock at night. Has 4s. a week. Would rather work fewer hours; but his father sends him, and takes the money.

6. Is fourteen years of age. Can write. Works at weaving and makes 5s. 6d. a week, working ten hours a day, and gives it to his aunt, who keeps him.

7. Is sixteen years of age. Works at factory, and has 6s. 2d. a week. Can write.

8. Is ten years of age. Works at a foundry for 13 hours a day, and earns 2s. 6d. a week, which his parents take.

9. Is ten years of age, and in a warehouse from half-past eight in the morning until eight o'clock at night. Learned to write here. Can make 3s. a week.

10. Is fourteen years of age. Works at factory in the spinning room. Has 5s. 9d. a week, and his father gives him 2d. a week pocket money. Can write a little. His father pays his fees at a night school.

11. Is fifteen years of age. Works at a factory, and makes 14s. or 15s. a week. Pays it all to his father, who sometimes gives him a shilling or so. Works from a quarter past five, a.m. until seven p.m.

12. Is twelve years of age. Works for his father, who is a painter, and who gives him 6d. a week to spend. Goes to a night school, for which his father pays 5d. a week.

13. Is eleven years of age. Works in a stone-yard for twelve hours a day. Has 4s. a week. Goes to a night school.

14. Is thirteen years of age. Works for 4s. a week at a "making up" place. His father and mother give him 6d. a week for pocket money. Buys "a many things."

15. Is eight years of age, and does not go out to work. Goes to school Sundays and week days.

16. Is eleven years of age. Works in a foundry from seven o'clock a.m. until eight or nine o'clock. Has 2s. 6d. a week.

The reader will perceive, from the above particulars, that boys are commonly employed in branches of trade, many of them of a laborious nature, for several hours a day longer than the term during which they could be legally employed in factories; and for a much smaller amount of wages than they would earn in the different processes of the cotton trade. In this one class were boys earning from 6s. to 7s. in factories, whilst those employed as workers in iron did not make much more than half the money. It must be borne in mind, however, that the future prospects of the young mechanics are better than those of the young spinners and weavers.

In the afternoon I visited a very large Dissenting Sunday school, connected with the Independent body – that attached to the Hope chapel in Salford. In this school it is not uncommon to see assembled, on one Sunday, three generations of the same family – children, their parents, and their grand-parents. There are three large school-rooms for the youthful scholars – from those who are mere children up to those of 18 or 20 years of age and separate rooms for the adult scholars of both sexes. The male adult class is managed by Mr. William Morris, the principal partner in a very large cotton-working establishment. Mr. Morris, who is one of the most respected citizens of Manchester, and who is justly proud of having worked himself up "from the ranks", takes the deepest practical interest in the Sunday school and temperance movements, and is a distinguished advocate of both causes. He passes many hours every Sunday, surrounded by his adult class, in the Hope chapel. The total number of pupils taught in those schools is about 1,200, and the average afternoon attendance is about 924. There are 160 in the infant class, and about 600 above fourteen years of age. More than 100 of the pupils are married persons. The absentee children are visited by the teachers. In the day school connected with the Hope chapel there are about 300 scholars. To the sick relief fund there are about 100 subscribers. and to a clothing charity about 530. This school raises annually about £50 for missionary purposes. The number of adult scholars taught separately is about 250.

In the library there are nearly 1,000 volumes, consisting principally of books of a serious character, and including a number of religious and controversial novels. The books in the Bennett Street school library are of the same general class, and number about twice as many. Upon neither of these libraries did the Ten Hours Bill produce any perceptible change.

In general intelligence and acquirements the children of both the St. Paul's and the Hope schools seemed pretty much upon a par. The children from ten to twelve years of age were able to read with tolerable fluency and correctness. After hearing one of the reading classes, I proceeded to examine into the social position and standing of the scholars, as at the Paul's school, and with the following results:

GIRLS

1. Is fifteen years of age. Works in a silk mill, and earns 3s. 5d. per week, which she gives to her parents. Can read and write.

2. Is fifteen years of age. Works in a weaving room, and earns 5s. 2d. a week. Her parents allowed her the odd twopence for herself, and she put a penny of it weekly into the missionary box.

3. Is thirteen years of age, and earns 2s. 3 ½d. per week at winding cotton. Has no pocket money.

4. Is sixteen years of age, and works as a piecer. Her wages are 8s. a week. Gives the money to a married sister with whom she lives, except twopence or three pence for herself. Can read and write.

Two girls, respectively seventeen and nineteen, who earned 10s. each as weavers, would not tell me what they did with the money.

BOYS

1. Is ten years of age. Works at a brick-croft as long as there is light. Has 2s. 6d. a week.

2. Is sixteen years of age. Works at a dye-house, where he has 6s. 6d. a week. His mother gives him 3d. or 4d. every Saturday night, and he spends it in sweet stuff. Can't read much.

3. Is twelve years of age. Works with a joiner for 2s. a week. Is learning to read. Works more than twelve hours a day very often.

4. Is fifteen years of age. Works with an umbrella frame maker and has 1s. 6d. a week, which he pays to his father. Has no pocket money.

5. Is fourteen years of age. Makes 5s. a week at a bleaching field. Gives the money to his parents, and has 6d. a week to do what he likes with. Buys fruit and sweet stuff.

6. Is fourteen years of age. Can read well. Works at a brick croft from dark to dark, for which he has 5s. a week.

7. Is sixteen year of age. Can read and write. Earns 12s. a week in a silk factory, and gives it to his old mother, except 6d., which he spends himself.

8. Is fifteen years of age. Works at a bleach field, where he has 14s. every fortnight. Gives it to his aunt. Is going to a night school, to learn to read and write, as soon as possible.

9. Is fourteen years of age, and has 4s. a week at a warehouse. Is allowed 3d. for pocket money. Can read and write.

10. Is seventeen years of age. Makes 6s. a week as a piecer. Gives it to his mother, except 4d., which he keeps himself.

The remark as to the length of employment of "children and young persons" in occupations not connected with factories, made apropos of the pupils of the Bennett Street school, stands also good in the present case. I am informed that very young children are frequently employed in the brick crofts, or fields, for fourteen hours a day in summer, and that the number of them has increased since the Ten Hours Act came into operation. I have no reason to doubt the accuracy of the statements made by the Sunday scholars as to their giving their wages almost entirely to their parents; and the inference which one would naturally draw from the fact, knowing what we do of the general practice, is, that the Sunday school system has, to some extent, the effect of discouraging the generally speedy rupture of the family tie. I now pass to another subject, only pausing to remark that the ages of the boys, as stated by themselves, astounded me. From their appearances, I should have thought them, on an average, at least three years younger than they represented themselves to be.

10. Lodging Houses

BEFORE going to see the vagrant lodging-houses in Manchester, I proceeded to inspect the model lodging-house recently established there. It is situated in the low and populous district of Ancoats, and was once the suburban mansion of the proprietor of a large neighbouring mill. It was curious to contrast the splendid sweep of the staircases, the mahogany doors, the rich cornices, and massy marble chimney pieces of many of the rooms with the style of the new fittings and the appearance of the inhabitants. We first went into the common dining-room. It was filled with plain clean deal tables and benches. It was after the general dinner hour in Manchester, and the few who had taken that meal in the house were gone. Two decent-looking young men only remained, smoking their pipes by the fire. In the "larder" are 40 cupboards, shut in by doors of perforated zinc, and so situated as to be exposed to a cool through draft. Each lodger pays 1s. for his key, and when he leaves the money is returned. The lodgers cook their own meals in the kitchen, where fuel and cooking apparatus is found them. Two men were engaged by the range in frying beefsteaks, when I was in the room. The apartment was perfectly sweet and cleanly. The dishes were washed in an adjacent scullery. The bedrooms were somewhat like the wards of hospitals, but the beds were placed fully six feet apart from each other. They are spread on compact iron bedsteads; the material is flock, and there are coarse but clean linen sheets, blankets, and a coverlid. By the head of each bed is a square box for the occupant's clothes. Many lodgers, however, had trunks of their own besides. In one of the bed wards, partitions six feet high have been built, inclosing each bed, and forming a series of little chambers, each about the size of what is called a state room on board ship. As these partitions are screens rather than walls, the ventilation is not materially interfered with, while a proper degree of isolation is produced. It is probable that this arrangement will be made general. The superintendent, a very obliging person, showed me four beds in one of the upper rooms, which were being arranged for four young men of a religious turn, who wished to be accommodated together. Let me not omit that there are washing rooms, with plenty of water, copper basons and jack towels, a bathroom, where the lodgers can have each, in turn, a plunge into hot water, and a large enclosed yard behind, which is to be made into a gymnasium. The establishment has been open only eight weeks. It commenced with fifteen or sixteen lodgers, and has gone on slowly increasing in number. The accommodation provided is at present for forty. The charge to each lodger is 2s. a week. For this he has a comfortable bed, conveniences for washing, cooking, eating his meals, and perfect and wholesome cleanliness. The charge for a single night is 4d. Many of the lodgers only sleep in the house, taking their meals abroad. The occupants are principally mechanics. There are blacksmiths, joiners, ribbon makers, three mill hands only, a schoolmaster, and a doctor.

Having thus seen the decent and wholesome lodging which a poor man may have for a sum which amounts to a very little more than the sixth of the average weekly earnings of an adult in Manchester, I proceeded to visit the lodgings which many of the poor but generally speaking, of course, the exceptional classes, earning precarious livelihoods, do occupy.

The lowest, most filthy, most unhealthy, and most wicked locality in Manchester is called, singularly enough, Angel-meadow. It lies off the Oldham-road, is full of cellars, and inhabited by prostitutes, their bullies, thieves, cadgers, vagrants, tramps, and, in the very worst sties of filth and darkness, by those unhappy wretches the "low Irish". My guide was a sub-inspector of police, an excellent conductor in one respect, but disadvantageous in another, seeing that his presence spread panic wherever he went. Many of the people visited that night had, doubtless, ample cause to be nervous touching the Presence of one of the guardians of the law.

We first went into an ordinary "low lodging house". The hour, I should state, was about nine o'clock at night. A stout man, partially undressed, was sitting, nursing a child, upon the bed of the outer room, and the landlady emerged from the inner apartment, whence followed her a great clack of male and female tongues. The woman spoke with profound deference to my companion, and began to assure him that the house was the best conducted in all Manchester. Meantime we had entered the inner room. It was a small stiflingly hot place, with a large fire, over which flickered a rush-light, or very small candle, stuck in a greased tin sconce. There were eight or ten men and women seated on stools and low chairs round the fire. They had been talking loudly enough a minute ago, but on our entrance they became as mute as fishes, staring stolidly into the fire, and only casting furtive glances at my companion and nodding to each other when his back was turned. Hot as the place was, most of the women had shawls about their heads. They were coarse-looking and repulsive – more than one with contused and discoloured faces. The men were of a class you often remark in low localities – squalid hulking fellows, with no particular mark of any trade or calling on them. The women were of the worst class of prostitutes, and the men their bullies and partners in robberies. The beds upstairs were broken and rickety, and clothes which were bundles of brown rags. These couches were placed so close that you could only just make your way between them. The regular charge was fourpence a bed. The landlady stoutly asserted that only two were allowed to sleep in each bed, but as to the sexes she was "noways particular – lodgers was lodgers, whether they was men or women". In the room in which we stood, and which might be about fourteen feet by twelve, more than a score of filthy vagrants often pigged together, dressed and undressed, sick and well, sober and drunk.

These lodging-houses are under the superintendence of the police, and only a certain number of beds are allowed to be in a room. But the law is continually violated. "Shake-downs" are made on the floor, and threes and fours crammed into the same bed. In another lodging-house my companion suddenly exclaimed to the landlady, "Why, here's a bed more than you are licensed for," pointing to a bundle of straw enclosed in a piece of coarse sacking and set upright in a corner. "Guide us a'," answered the woman in the richest *patois* of the Canongate, "guide us a', what's the body havering about ? It's my ain bed, man. Ye wad na hae me sleep on the stanes? But we'se remove it, if that be a';" and so saying, she caught up her couch and trundled it downstairs.

"Where do you generally sleep?" I said. "Oh, just ony gate. It depends on whether the hoose is full – but or ben, or in the passage or ony gate."

The nominal price of fourpence for a bed I found to be everywhere the same, and the general disposition of the bedrooms was equally identical. They consist simply of filthy unscoured chambers, with stained and discoloured walls, scribbled over with names and foul expressions. Sometimes the plaster had fallen, and lay in heaps in the corners. There was no article of furniture other than the beds – not even, so far as I saw, a chest. Still the worst of the places was quite weather-tight.

One street in this quarter is entirely composed of lodging-houses, and is well known to the police throughout the kingdom. It was called Blakely Street, but now goes by the name of Charter Street. There is a tavern here, with a coloured lamp like that of a doctor's, called the "Dog and Duck". This is the house of call for the swell mob of Manchester and the superior class of "prigs".[1] When I entered the parlour, which differed in no respect from that of an ordinary low-class tavern, and which was hung with boxing prints, there were only two men present, drinking ale, and playing dominos for handfuls of coppers. In a beer-house close at hand there was a large assemblage of men and women, most of the latter like those I have already sketched, but a few whose faded finery proclaimed that they had formerly held a higher position in their wretched class. A number of bare-footed boys were drinking here. The rattle of dominos was heard on every side: the yellow dips which lighted the room burned with a sickly flicker amid the draughts and the thick tobacco smoke. Ensconced in the

---

[1] Prigs – thieves.

seat of honour by the fire was a villainous-looking black man without shoes, who said that he had just come to town, having "cadged it from Stafford"; and in a corner sat two pedlars, each upon his box. As we were leaving the house a boy about thirteen or fourteen, smartly dressed, with a tassel dangling from his cap, entered.

"Well, young 'un," said my companion, "Whose pockets have your hands been in this evening?"

The boy stared coolly at the inspector. The light from a lamp fell on his face, and I never saw a worse one – little deep-sunk eyes, and square bony jaws, with a vile expression. "What do you mean talking about pockets to me? I don't know nothing about pockets," and turning on his heel he entered the house. The boy had been twice convicted, and several times in trouble. He walked Market-street at night, often in partnership with a woman.

There were few or no Irish in the houses we had just visited. They live in more wretched places still – the cellars. We descended to one. The place was dark, except for the glare of a small fire. You could not stand without stooping in the room, which might be about twelve feet by eight. There were at least a dozen men, women and children on stools, or squatted on the stone floor, round the fire, and the heat and smells were oppressive. This not being a lodging cellar, the police had no control over the number of its inmates, who slept huddled on the stones, or on masses of rags, shavings and straw, which were littered about. There was nothing like a bedstead in the place. Further back opened a second cellar, strewn with coats and splinters of wood used for making matches. Here, upon shavings, bits of furze, and intermingled rags and straw, lay two girls asleep in two corners. The party in the outer room had a few handfuls of nuts and apples with which they intended – it was the 31st October – to "keep" All Hallow's Eve. Half the people who lived in the den had not yet returned, being still out hawking lucifers, matches and besoms. They were all Irish, from Westport, in the county of Mayo. They lived on potatoes, meal, and sometimes broken victuals begged. There was no fever there, and there had been no cholera – "Glory be to God". "Sure they was poor people, but they was daysint and did their best." After leaving, a woman followed me into the street to know if I had come from Westport to find out anything about them, and was greatly disappointed at being answered in the negative.

The last place we visited is, I am told, the worst cellar in all Manchester. The outer room was like that of others which I had seen, but following a woman who held a light, we proceeded into the inner cellars. They were literally vaults, three of them opening from one to the other. The air was thick with damp and stench. The vaults were mere subterranean holes, utterly without light. The flicker of the candle showed their grimy walls, reeking with foetid damp, which trickled in greasy drops down to the floor. Beds were huddled in every corner: some of them on frames – I cannot call them bedsteads – others on the floor. In one of these a man was lying dressed, and beside him slept a well-grown calf. Sitting upon another bed was an old man maudlin drunk, with the saliva running over his chin, making vain efforts to rid himself of his trowsers, and roaring for help. In the next cellar two boys were snoring together in one bed, and beside them was a man sleeping in an old battered hat for a nightcap. "Is he undressed?" I said. The police officer, for answer, twitched down the clothes, and revealed a stark naked man, black with filth. The smell in this room was dreadful, and the air at once hot and wet.

"What's this you have been doing?" said my conductor to the landlady, stooping down and examining the lower part of one of the walls. I joined him, and saw that a sort of hole or shallow cave, about six feet long, two deep, and a little more than one high, had been scooped out through the wall into the earth on the outside of the foundation, there being probably some yard on the other side, and in this hole or earthen cupboard there was stretched, upon a scanty litter of foul-smelling straw, a human being – an old man. As he lay on his back, his face was not two inches beneath the roof – so to speak – of the hole.

"He's a poor old body," said the landlady, in a tone of deprecation, "and if we didn't let him crawl in there he would have to sleep in the streets."

I turned away, and was glad when I found myself breathing such comparatively fresh air as can be found in Angel Meadow, Manchester.

11. Music and Music Halls

MANCHESTER is known as being of late years a decidedly musical place. Since the passing of the Ten Hours Bill, a great Monday night concert for the operative classes has been in successful operation. I visited it the other night. The musical attractions, to be sure, were rather mild – a small organ, a piano, an amateur chorus of some thirty voices, assisted by a few professors of only local celebrity. But the programme comprised selections from Handel, Meyerbeer, Rossini and Bishop; and if these were at the best only respectably performed, they were listened to with the most reverent silence, and then applauded to the echo by an assemblage of between two and three thousand working men and women, who had respectively paid their three pence for admission, and who took up nearly the entire area of the Free Trade Hall.

Interior of the Free Trade Hall, Peter Street, 1865

The first encore was won by Handel's beautiful melody, "Oh, had I Jubal's Lyre", and to prove how catholic were the sympathies of the audience, they broke out into raptures when the vocalist, upon being recalled, substituted for the Handelian melody "Jeannette and Jeannot". If the concert were not a musical phenomenon, it was at all events a moral one.

Let me try to describe a curiously characteristic place of amusement which I visited the other day in Manchester. I was anxious to see and judge of for myself one of the music saloons, of which I had heard so much; and so, ascertaining that the Apollo in the London-road presented a very good specimen, I waited until Saturday night should exhibit it in its greatest glory, and then set off for the hall of jollity and harmony. The London Road is full of cheap shops devoted to the sale of ordinary household matters. Stalls, covered and uncovered, heaped over with still coarser and cheaper wares, abound. Gas flares blazed amid the joints in the butchers' open shops. Faintly burning candies, enclosed in greasy paper lanterns, cast their dim and tallowy influence over tables slimy with cheap fish, or costermongers' barrows littered with cabbages or apples. The gin-shops are in full feather – their swinging doors never hang a moment still. Itinerant bands blow and bang their loudest; organ boys grind monotonously; ballad singers or flying stationers make roaring proclamations of their wares. The street is one swarming, buzzing mass of people. Boys and girls shout and laugh and disappear into the taverns together. Careful housewives – often attended by their husbands dutifully carrying the baby – bargain hard with the butchers for a halfpenny off in the pound. In a cheap draper's shop, a committee of young women will be examining into the merits of a dress which one of them has determined to buy; while, in an underground pie-shop, a select party of juveniles will be regaling themselves upon musty pasties of fat pork. The pawnbroker is busy, for pledges are being rapidly redeemed, and flat irons, dirty pairs of stays, candlesticks, Sunday trowsers, tools, blankets, and so forth, are fast being removed from his shelves. The baker has chalked on a black board, in his boldest characters, "Down again to even money – a four-pound loaf for five pence." Here a woman is anxiously attempting – half to drive, half to lure home her drunken husband; there a couple of tipsy fellows are in high dispute, their tobacco pipes in their hands, and a noisy circle of backers urging them on. From byways and alleys and back streets, fresh crowds every moment emerge. Stalls, shops, cellars are clustered round with critics or purchasers – cabmen drive slowly through the throng, shouting and swearing to the people to get out of the horse's way; and occasionally, perhaps, the melodious burst of a roaring chorus, surging out of the open windows of the Apollo, resounds loudly above the whole conglomeration of street noises.

A bright lamp over an open door points out the entrance to lovers of harmony and beer. Here there is a check-taker, helped, and no doubt superintended, by a policeman, who will not allow drunken people to pass. An intimation stares you in the face that, in order to "keep the company select", a charge of twopence is made, on the payment of which a ticket will be given, entitling the bearer to two pennyworth of refreshments upstairs. Having complied with the terms of this reasonable proposition, you mount a broad steep staircase, and presently find yourself at the extremity of a long narrow room. On the occasion of my first appearance on the scene, the place was densely crowded by men and women, and the air was one roiling volume of tobacco smoke. I thought that to obtain a seat was out of the question, but a bustling personage, whom I soon found to be the landlord, was very busy packing away his guests into the smallest possible compass; and at length, he accommodated me with six inches of a bench, and about two square inches of a table on which to place the tumbler of porter – and not bad it was – to which my two penny coupon entitled me. I have said that the room was long and narrow. The walls were covered with paper representing carved woodwork. About midway on one side was a small bar, where the landlady was drawing ale and beer, the only liquors for which the house was licensed. Along the length of the apartment ran curiously narrow tables, with benches on either side, placed so close to each other, and occupied by such a dense swarm of people as to make it all but impossible for the female waiters to hand the malt liquor about, and accordingly the tumblers were often passed along from hand to hand. At the upper end of the place was a small stage, with a regular proscenium, built *secundem artem*, but so low that the performers' heads almost touched the "flies". Upon the stage was what is technically called a "set scene" of a cottage and a landscape. Beneath was an orchestra, consisting of two or three fiddles and a pianoforte. Of the audience, two-thirds might be men; the others were women – young and old – a few of them with children seated in their laps, and several with babies at their breasts. The class of the assembly was that of artisans and mill-hands. Almost without an exception, men and women were decently dressed, and it was quite evident that several of the groups formed family parties. When I entered, a man, dressed in the conventional "nigger" costume, was singing one of those really pretty airs which have of late gained such popular renown, and singing it, too, with much feeling for the melody and less regard for the slang part of the business than are generally exhibited by London performers of a similar class. The audience joined in the chorus *con amore*, so that, just as I entered, nearly two hundred voices, male and female, were entreating Susanna not to cry for the minstrel who was "going to Alabama with his banjo on his knee".

I stayed nearly an hour, heard half-a-dozen songs, and witnessed a couple of dances. The former were chiefly of that class happily characterized by Mr. Thackeray as the "British Brandy-and-Water School". One of the whole number was objectionable from its double *entendres*, but it was vehemently applauded and uproariously enjoyed. The only female performer was a little girl about twelve, who sang a "Medley song", and danced a *pas* to correspond. The other saltatory artist was a young man who, dressed as a soldier, went through a sort of parody of the manual exercise, and then swinging round, exhibited himself with a mask tied to the back of his head, and his rear "made up" for the front of a theatrical sailor, in which character he performed a most energetic hornpipe.

"He's a clever chap, is that," said a little dirty-faced man to me.

"Indeed!"

"Aye, he is. Why, sir, he works in factory with me."

There was no answering such conclusive criticism. I asked the connoisseur whether the other performers were also factory hands? No; they were all mere "arteests", save the hornpipe man. So far as I saw, the company were quite as decorous as could be expected for a convivial assemblage of their rank. There was plenty of loud speaking, and now and then coarse speaking; but there was nobody drunk – an assertion which, however, I fear would hardly stand good a couple of hours afterwards. The only person who seemed inclined to be riotous and unruly was a middle-aged woman who had taken more porter than was good for her; and, what appeared to me worse, was successfully encouraging two young girls, whom she had brought with her, to do the same – vehemently expressing all the time her admiration at the masculine beauties of the bass singer, and repeatedly demanding (with reference to the gentleman in question) whether I had "ever seen such a lovely nose on a face?"

Another evening I went to a favourite musical place in another part of the town, at the corner of the Oldham Road. Unhappily I had mistaken the harmonic night; but the landlord, to whom I explained my business, showed me the curious arrangements by means of which he manages to have the same performance in two rooms at once. There are two spacious apartments directly over each other. The floor of the upper, and the ceiling of the lower are perforated with a great square aperture like a hatchway in a deck. This vast trap can be covered or revealed by two flaps, which, when they are lifted, are secured back to back in the centre. In the upper room, upon a little platform on the brink of the gulf, the vocal performers stand, so as to be seen by all the audience in their own room and by about one half of those in the lower room, in which again just beneath the feet of the artists, is placed an extremely handsome barrel organ, the front consisting of plate glass, and exhibiting its musical snuff-box like machinery, and which can be seen by all the guests in the lower room and a few of those in the higher room. Thus the musical attractions are made as impartial as possible. The organ cost £194. The landlord wound it up for my benefit, and it went off with good effect into the overture of *William Tell*.

On my way home that night, I looked into two additional places of popular amusement. One was a sleight-of-hand exhibition in a small room up a rickety flight of stairs. The charge was 2d., and the benches were occupied principally by young men and women, evidently mill hands. One boy, not above sixteen, sat between two girls, with an arm round each of their necks; while the Sultanas, who were evidently jealous, exchanged scowling glances as they cracked the hazel nuts which all three were occupied in demolishing. The others of the company sat quietly enough. There were two elderly women, in faded shawls and limp bonnets, gravely discussing how the magical tricks were performed. Near them sat two young women, nursery maids apparently, with young children on their knees, and a sprinkling of grown-up men, with folded-up carpenters' rules protruding from their pockets and bespeaking their occupation, formed a party of their own. There was music, in the shape of a flageolet and fife, blown by two men seated at the end of the audience benches, while a lout of a boy in shoes, with wooden soles an inch thick, danced a Lancashire clog hornpipe, keeping up a monotonous rattle with his wooden-shod feet. At first I looked upon the young gentleman as an amateur, his performance being conducted in the audience part of the room; but from the unvarying clatter which he produced during the interval between any sleight-of-hand, I found he was one of the artistes of the establishment.

The last place of "amusement" which I visited was a gratis concert-room, but frequented by a better class than the attendants at the Apollo, many of the persons present being evidently mechanics from the neighbouring Atlas Iron Works.[1] There were also women in the room, all of them, apparently, in their own fashion, respectable. The room was a comfortable one, with oil paintings, one representing the Vale of Tempe "in Italy." There was a piano and some wretched sentimental singing, during which the *habitués* grimly smoked and drank their spirits and water. I soon beat a retreat from such dull quarters.

In returning last Sunday night, by the Oldham Road, from one of my tours, I was somewhat surprised to hear the loud sounds of music and jollity which floated out of the public-house windows. The street was swarming with drunken men and women; and with young mill girls and boys shouting, hallooing and romping with each other. Now I am not one of those who look upon the slightest degree of social indulgence as a downright evil, but I confess that last Sunday night in the Oldham Road astonished and grieved me. In no city have I ever witnessed a scene of more open, brutal, and general intemperance. The public-houses and gin-shops were roaring full. Rows, and fights, and scuffles were every moment taking place within doors and in the streets. The whole street rung with shouting, screaming, and swearing, mingled with the jarring music of half-a-dozen bands. A tolerably intimate acquaintance with most phases of London life enables me to state that in no part of the metropolis would the police have tolerated such a state of things for a single Sunday. I entered one

---

[1] Run by Sharp Brothers and Co. in Great Bridgewater Street.

of the musical taverns – one of the best of them. It was crowded to the door with men and women – many of them appearing to belong to a better station in life than mill hands or mechanics. The music consisted of performances on the piano and seraphine.[1] In the street I accosted a policeman, telling him of my surprise that music should be allowed in public-houses on Sunday evenings. Such a thing was never dreamt of in London.

"Oh," quoth he, "there is an understanding that they don't play nothing but sacred music."

"Sacred music," I said. "Well, it is the first time I ever heard the 'Bay of Biscay' and the 'Drum Polka' invested with the title."

---

[1] Seraphine – an early type of harmonium.

THE ASHWORTHS OF EGERTON

A "RURAL FACTORY!" To how many will the phrase seem a contradiction in terms! In the minds of how many are even the best features of the cotton-mill associated with the worst features of a squalid town. And yet, thickly sprinkled amid the oak-coppiced vales of Lancashire with the whitewashed cottages of the workpeople gleaming through the branches and beside the rapid stream, or perched high on the breezy forehead of the hill, are to be seen hundreds on hundreds of busily working cotton mills. In the vicinity of these are no foetid alleys, no grimy courts, no dark area or underground cellars. Even the smoke from the tall chimneys passes tolerably innocuously away – sometimes, perhaps, when the air is calm and heavy, dotting the grass or the leaves with copious showers of "blacks", but never serious smirching nor blighting the dewy freshness of the fields and hedgerows, through which the spinner and the weaver pass to their daily toil.

I visited the other day the country factory of Egerton, belonging to the Messrs. Ashworth, and situated a few miles to the north of Bolton.[1] The railway from Manchester to the latter town spans ten miles of open breezy country, dotted here and there with mills or calico works snugly nestled in the valleys – amid meadow and pasture land and pleasant hardwood coppices – the eye not failing here and there to catch the antique outline of a clumsily picturesque farmhouse which has looked forth from amid its sheltering trees

---

[1] For a history of the firm and the impressions of other visitors, see Rhodes Boyson, *The Ashworth Cotton Enterprise*, Oxford, 1970.

since the days when Bolton was a petty hamlet, and Manchester a handful of straggling streets. The former town is as bad a specimen of a nucleus of cotton manufacturers as can be conceived. It is an old spinning and weaving station, and the great mass of the houses are built in the oldest and filthiest fashion. Cellars abound on every side, and I saw few or none unoccupied, while the people appeared to me to be fully as squalid and dirty in appearance as the worst classes are in the worst districts of Manchester. Bolton is inhabited by what in this part of the country is known as an "old" population – a population which in a great degree preserves hurtful old prejudices and filthy old fashions, which have little hold in the more modern seats of industry. In common with Stockport, the town of Bolton was awfully afflicted by the stagnations of business in 1842 and 1847. In the latter year, the unemployed population was supported at a weekly cost of from £100 to £500. And even at present, when trade is reasonably brisk, the weekly amount of poor-rates is nearly £230. The last poor-law return dated Somerset House, July 17, 1849, inform us that the number inmates of the Bolton workhouse on the 1st of July, 1848, was 41 while no less than 7,371 individuals had, up to that date in that year, received out-door relief.

The road to Egerton is full of beauties. It winds along the valley of the Eagley, a tributary of the Irwell, amidst pleasant meadow land, green grassy ridges, and sheltered ravines and dells running wantonly amid the tumbled hills. The oak seems an especial favourite of this hardy soil. Here and there are flourishing coppice-woods, green with the scolloped leaf of our national tree; and now and then you mark the grand branches and lichen-grown boll of a fine gnarled old fellow who has shed his leaves a hundred times. Every mile or so down in the valley beside the running stream lies a factory of some sort or other, often half-hidden by the sheltering trees; and further up the hill, upon the green slope you mark the decent row of substantial stone-built cottages, where the "hands" live. Churches with neat spires, and the more unpretending tabernacles of dissent, plain, capacious buildings, with "Sion" or "Bethesda" deeply carved over their simple lintels, bespeak the different shades of religious feeling of the district; while the handsome garden-circled mansions which you frequently pass remind you that the proprietors of the wealth-producing establishments around are rarely, if ever, absentees. Little or no corn is grown hereabouts. The ground is meadow land, for the pasture of horses and kine. Beneath the surface lie thick strata of coal, as the rude-looking mechanism, reared upon mounds of cinders and presiding over each by a short smoking chimney, will not fail to testify. The river you will observe, is frequently dammed back into ponds or "lodges", in order that the power which it supplies may be as much as possible husbanded, the mills here working by force both of hot water and cold; and the entire picture which we have been trying to reproduce is set in a frame of dusky hills, many of them heather covered and haunted by moor game.

The village of Egerton principally consists of a long street running along the highway. The Messrs. Ashworth's mills lie beneath it, at the bottom of a rather deep and wooded valley, and thither we will descend.

Factories abound little in architectural graces, but the country mills appear to far more advantage than their town brethren, inasmuch as all of them are clean-looking, some brightly whitewashed and others, in certain parts of the country, built of substantial grey stone. The mills at Egerton are of this last description. They are propelled by steam and water power, and a huge wheel for the latter purpose, sixty feet in diameter, is really one of the sights of Lancashire.

The waterwheel of Ashworth's Mill at Egerton, 1848

The number of hours worked at this establishment is eleven a day, and the time of labour at present commences at six o'clock. The general arrangements of cotton mills are very similar, but I can confidently speak of the excellent arrangements of the Messrs. Ashworth's establishment. The large card, roving and drawing room on the basement storey is fully eleven feet from floor to ceiling, and perfectly ventilated. The temperature was a few degrees higher than that of the atmosphere, but perfectly clear from the slightest degree of closeness or smell. The windows, too, are very large, and provided with full arrangements of swinging panes. The labour which was proceeding in this airy and well-arranged *atelier* was clearly of a nature which could have no prejudicial effect upon health; and the women looked very obviously better than those in the town mills. Their faces, in hardly a single instance, wore that thoroughly blanched hue which is an almost unvarying characteristic of the city cotton-spinners; while many of the girls had very perceptible roses in their cheeks. Their working dresses were scrupulously neat and upon the shoulder of each was embroidered the name of its proprietor.

The Messrs. Ashworth are in the constant and excellent habit of mingling familiarly and kindly with their workpeople, all of whom they are personally acquainted with. They do as much as they can to discourage the working of married women with young families in the mill – a practice which I confidently hope to be able to stigmatise as being, beyond cavil, infinitely the blackest plague spot on the whole of the manufacturing system. Not above four women of the class in question labour in Messrs. Ashworth's Egerton mills. The average wages in the country mills are a trifle below those paid in towns; but rent and provisions being usually lower in the rural districts, there is little virtual difference. Seven-eighths of Messrs. Ashworth's people live in cottages built upon their employer's land, but this is left to their free option. The rent of these cottages varies from 1s. 6d. to 3s. 6d. weekly. For the latter rent a labourer can possess a substantially built stone cottage, containing a good parlour and kitchen, two or three bedrooms, a cellar, and a small garden. The latter advantage is not, however, much in request among the Egerton workpeople. The amount of rent quoted is the sum total payable for the occupation of the house. It is generally deducted from the wages; but the tenancy being, as I have said, purely optional, there is no objectionable approach to the truck system in the transaction. I wish, however, I could say that this practice prevails universally. The case of certain mills in Bolton has been brought under my notice, in which the charge of a complement of spinning mules – the best operative situation in a cotton mill – is always clogged with the condition that the spinner shall live in a house belonging to the employer. In the workpeople's own phraseology, "a key goes to each set of mules". Now although I do not mean to say that the houses are not worth the rent charged, yet a spinner may be unmarried, and have no occasion for four or five rooms. I heard it stated, indeed, that in one instance in Bolton, a young man so situated sub-lets his house for sixpence a week to an individual who keeps pigs in it.

To return, however, to the Egerton mills. The cottages are not supplied with water in the interior, but there is plenty in the vicinity. The three-shilling houses have a bedroom less than the first-class cottages. There is a news-room attached to the mill, in which twelve papers, besides periodicals, are taken. For its support the operatives who frequent it pay a penny per week. There is also a library, numbering about 300 volumes. The children under thirteen years of age go as usual to school, and play one half of each day, and work the other half.

The village of Egerton, although inhabited solely by a factory population, is as sweet, wholesome, and smokeless as it could be were its denizens the most bucolic hinds of Devon. I wandered up and down its straggling streets. The houses are furnished much in the same fashion as those of the middling Manchester class; but every article of household use looks better, because cleaner and fresher. Here is no grime nor squalor. The people are hard-working labourers, but they live decently and fare wholesomely. There is no ragged wretchedness to be seen, no ruinous and squalid hovels. There are two taverns in the village – quiet, decent places. One of them, called the Globe, boasts of a sign which, I trust, may not lead astray the geographical wits of the rising generation of Egerton, seeing that the hydrographer has drawn the outline of Europe as encircling the South Pole. This by the way, however. There are no dram shops in Egerton, and no pawnbrokers. None of the people in the mill belong to any trades' combination, and there has been no turn-out since the village was a village. In the country around, hares and rabbits are plenty, but no poaching is heard of. The few agricultural labourers in the vicinity get, on the average, 12s. a week. For this they frequently labour 15 hours a day. They live in the farm houses with their employers. Altogether, the village of Egerton presents a gratifying spectacle of the manufacturing system working under favourable auspices. I was perfectly delighted with the healthy and ruddy looks of the young children. While I was lounging about, a caravan came toiling up hill, and the news of the arrival of the wonder-laden vehicle having quickly spread, the youngsters came swarming out of every cottage to wonder and admire – fine chubby, red-faced, white-headed urchins, the picture of health and good feeling. This very gratifying result I attribute partly to the pure air, but mostly to the mothers seldom or never labouring in the mill. It is the neglect of very young children at home, while their mothers toil in the factories, which causes nineteen-twentieths of the infant deaths in Manchester. The people of Egerton are described to me as being very healthy, and epidemics are rare amongst them. The late Dr. Cooke Taylor, in one of his able and interesting works on the factory system, gives a gratifying account of the morality of the mill population in the district, taking, as an index to the general feeling of respect for property, the case of the garden of the Messrs. Ashworth, which, although it was full of the finest fruit, perfectly unprotected, and passed every day by the mill hands, young and old, never suffered so much as the loss of a cherry or a flower.[1] This statement, from my own observations, I can readily believe. There are a number of country mills excellently ordered in the valley of Eagley. Conspicuous amongst these is the establishment of Mr. Bazley, the president of the Manchester Chamber of Commerce. This gentleman has constructed ranges of admirably built cottages, each of them supplied with water in the interior. A lecture-room, capable of accommodating 400 or 500 people, is one of the principle public buildings of this excellent operative colony.[2]

Returning to Bolton, I proceeded to visit the mill and cottages belonging to Messrs. Arrowsmith and Slater, upon the outskirts of the town.[3] The gentlemen in

---

[1] W. Cooke Taylor, *Notes of a tour in the manufacturing districts of Lancashire*, 2nd edn., London, Sept. 1842, footnote pp 23-24.

[2] Gardner and Bazley's factory settlement was at Barrow-bridge. It was visited by Prince Albert in 1851. See C. Aspin, *Lancashire, the first industrial society*, Helmshore, 1969, p. 137.

[3] In the Gilnow district.

question have taken the lead in Bolton in providing good accommodation, at reasonable rates, for their workpeople, having built two comfortable ranges of cottages, respectively called after Mr. Cobden and Mr. Bright, in which their spinners reside. Indeed, at present, Mr. Arrowsmith lives in one of these cottages himself. The houses are of two classes; the better sort have each a good front parlour, a light and spacious kitchen, a commodious pantry, a back yard with proper out-house conveniences; and above, two bedrooms. In the inferior class one room serves for parlour and kitchen, the second apartment on the ground floor being a sort of scullery or laundry. There was a small but handy range for cooking by each fireplace. The rent for a dwelling of this sort is 4s. 1d. per week – a sum which includes gas and water, both of which are laid on. In the cottage which I visited, dinner was just being got ready, and a dish of more savoury smelling Irish stew I have seldom encountered. On a slope stretching away from Cobden Terrace is about an acre and a half of ground, laid out in unfenced gardens, one of which belongs to each cottage. This summer, Mr. Arrowsmith gave his people prizes of engravings for the best shows of vegetables and flowers. The wane of autumn is a bad time for inspecting a garden, but I saw enough to satisfy me that the ground had been very carefully tilled, and a good harvest of vegetables reaped from it. I may add that, upon the occasion of a recent strike in Bolton, the turn-outs, although they tried hard, succeeded in only stopping for about two hours Messrs. Arrowsmith and Slater's Mill.

ASHTON-UNDER-LYNE

IN SELECTING the minor cotton towns round Manchester, which I think it my duty to visit, I try to fix upon those which present local peculiarities and distinct social characteristics. In general, indeed, these towns wear a monotonous sameness of aspect, physical and moral. The rates of wages paid are nearly on a par – the prices of the commodities for which they are spent are nearly on a par – the toil of the people at the mills, and their habits and arrangements at home, are all but identical. In fact, the social condition of the different town populations is almost as much alike as the material appearance of the tall chimneys under which they live. Here and there the height of the latter may differ by a few rounds of brick, but, in all essential respects, a description of one is a description of all.

In searching, however, for minor shades of social distinction, I find some two or three characteristics which separate Ashton-under-Lyne from its spinning neighbours – and which may excuse me for making it the main subject of a letter. Ashton is occupied by a "new" population, and, in some respects, it is as much a model cotton working town as any we have. The nucleus of the place is indeed old, filthy and dilapidated in the extreme; but nine-tenths of the town owes its existence immediately to the power-loom, and, in nearly all that large proportion, the houses are more comfortable, the streets more open, and better drained than in the great majority of industrial Lancashire towns.

Ashton lies about seven miles from Manchester, and directly "under" the "Lyne", of that long healthy ridge of hills called the "Backbone of England" – a chain which, under the local name of Blackstone Edge, separates Lancaster from York, and then runs northward through Westmoreland and Northumberland, until it loses itself among the undulations of the Scottish Cheviots. Ashton is built upon the banks of the Tame, a stream rising in the Yorkshire moors. The country around is level and bleak, the soil marshy and cold. In 1841, the population of the town was 24,000; at present it is over 34,000. The mills about Ashton are very generally the property of large capitalists, who can afford, and often do afford, to employ their people at full hours when a period of temporary slackness in trade obliges those masters whose command of capital is less at once to curtail their producing operations. In this respect Ashton is the reverse of Oldham. In the latter town small capitalists abound. It is not, indeed, uncommon there for several masters to unite to rent a mill, and sometimes to unite to rent even the floor of a mill. These employers conduct their operations in the hand-to-mouth style which naturally follows from such a state of things. They spin, moreover, generally speaking, the coarse and inferior kinds of thread, and the slightest check in the demand falls at once upon the workman. There is no shield of capital to stand between the humble producer and the immediate fluctuations of the market. From what reason I know not, but no returns of the pauperism of Oldham are given in the last tabular statistics presented by the Somerset House Board to Parliament; but I was informed by Mr. Tipping, the active and very intelligent relieving officer of Ashton, that an estimate had been constructed, showing the relative amount of pauperism at Oldham to be nearly double that at Ashton. The latter union contains a population of 101,000, and includes one or two small hamlets. The amount at present paid by the guardians is about £125 weekly for out-door relief, while there are in the workhouse about 200 inmates. I may add that the locality has been very slightly visited by cholera – only about thirty deaths having taken place throughout the union.

The population of Ashton have the reputation of being turbulent and fanatical. A policeman was killed in a disturbance here lately. The most ultra-political and theological opinions run riot amongst the population. The only manifest opposition which I have observed to the late day of humiliation[1] was in Ashton, where the dead walls were covered with placards denouncing the "Humbug", but adding, and Heaven knows with much truth, that the people want feasts quite as much as fasts. Ashton, too, is still the stronghold of the Southcote faith. A handsome row of grocers' shops, with long-bearded men behind the counters, was pointed out to me as a sort of colony of the people who still hold the strange creed in question. There is a "New Jerusalem", too, in which the faithful still meet. It is a substantial stone building, with the words, "The Sanctuary of Israel", flanked by two Hebrew mottoes, carved upon the wall. Indeed, what *La Vendee* was to Louis XVI, Ashton was to Johanna Southcote. Her labourers there mustered sturdiest, strongest. They proposed to enclose the town within a square wall, and actually did build four large houses

---

[1] The towns and cities of Britain reacted to the cholera epidemic of 1849 by observing "days of humiliation." That at Ashton was on October 24, when, according to newspaper reports, "the churches and other places of worship were open and attended by devout, if not very numerous congregations." Some mill owners, however, "did not see fit to close their establishments."

three of which are still standing, and which were intended to form the corners of the barrier.

The chief disciple in Ashton was a Mr. Wroe. He established a "Treasury of the Lord", constituted himself the treasurer, and supplies poured in fast from those who wished to have an investment at once in earth and Heaven. Many families were thus ruined at Ashton. At length the leader of the sect, having fallen into bad odour with his brethren, was tried in the New Jerusalem, whither repaired the chief man of the congregation, armed with a horsewhip. Before the reading of the list of imputed iniquities was half over, the accused tried to bolt out of the chapel. The denouncer followed his pastor, whip in hand; but Wroe having partisans, his pursuer was seized, a battle royal ensued, pews and seats were splintered, beards torn out by handfuls, and at length the police were obliged to clear the New Jerusalem. Notwithstanding the scandal of such events, the Faith was not overturned and, as I have hinted, the flowing beard of a "Johanna", as a disciple is called in Ashton, is still very common in the streets.[1]

In Ashton, too, there lingers on a handful of miserable old men, the remnants of the cotton hand-loom weavers. No young persons think of pursuing such an occupation – the few who practise it were too old and confirmed in old habits, when the power-loom was introduced, to be able to learn a new way of making their bread. The Ashton hand-loom weavers live, almost to a man, in the old, filthy, and undrained parts of the town. I begged Mr Tipping, the relieving officer who was good enough to be my cicerone, to enable me to see what he would consider a fair specimen of the class. We repaired therefore to one of the oldest portions of the place, called Charleston. The streets thereabouts were filthy and mean, the houses crumbling, crazy, and dirty. We threaded a labyrinth of noisome courts and small airless squares, formed generally of houses of a fair size, but miserably out of repair, slatternly women lounging about the thresholds; and neglected, dirty-faced children sprawling and roaring in the gutters. The door of one of these houses stood open, showing a steep, dark staircase,

---

[1] Johanna Southcote (1750-1814), a Methodist servant girl from Devonshire, who believed she received messages from Heaven and who prophesied that she would bear a child, the Prince of Peace. She died two months before the date fixed for the child's birth. John Wroe (1782-1863) founded the Christian Israelites, a sect which still flourishes in the United States. The male adherents followed Wroe in growing their beards to Biblical dimensions.

black with mud. The plaster had fallen in lumps from the wall, showing the lath beneath, and the coating which remained seemed covered with a dark greasy slime. Up this staircase we proceeded, and at the top turned into a bare room, the picture of squalid desolation. The chamber was a large one, but hardly an article did it contain which could be by courtesy denominated furniture. The principal objects were the loom and the bed. The latter had, to my eye, the appearance of a large square frame about seven feet long, and at least four broad, filled with sacking, upon which lay a single blanket recently given by the workhouse, and a chaos of miserable articles of dress – bundles of rags, in fact, which appeared to 'be used as additional coverings. Upon lines stretching across the room hung tattered morsels of under-clothing. There was one small round deal table and two or three broken old chairs, but the whole place was littered with an indescribable chaos of dirty odds and ends, bits of broken pewter, spoons, fragments of plates – here a rusty old breakfast knife, there a dry blacking -bottle, there a strip of stained and torn calico. On a low chair, by the small fire, sat a woman, looking one bundle of dingy tatters, bending over the hearth, and busily employed in some job of needle-work, while she rocked herself to and fro to lull the child which clung to her bosom. Another child was sprawling on the floor, playing with a large brown and white rabbit, which scampered about the place, frisking among the treddles of the loom. By the latter stood the weaver. He was a gaunt, big-boned man, with a stony glare in his eyes, and a rigid unimpassioned looking face, on which was stamped the most unequivocal marks of a stolid, hopeless, apathetic despair. The man was preparing hanks from which to produce a mingled web of linen and wool. He went about it like one half torpid, and who works from mere instinct, without energy and without hope.

I asked him what were his usual wages.

"Not five shillings a week."

"Your trade is a bad one now?"

He made no reply for a moment, but presently said, in a low drawling tone, and with a sort of strange smile on his face, as if he enjoyed the recital of the very hopelessness of his condition:

"Look here – I'll have to weave eighty yards of cloth in this piece. It will take me eight or nine days, and I shall have seven shillings for it. I walked to Manchester and back to the master's to fetch the yarn, and I shall walk there and back with the cloth when I am paid."

Here was a journey on foot amounting to nearly thirty miles, and nine days' work at the loom, for seven shillings!

The family consisted of four. They all slept together in the bed of sacking and rags. The rent of the room was one shilling per week, which the parish paid. Some of the hand-loom weavers are better off, because they have sons and daughters who work in the mills; but, taken all together, they are a wretched and hopeless set. Potatoes and bread, with a little miserably weak tea, form, of course, the only articles of nutriment which they ever taste.

The trade of the hatter was once a flourishing one both in Manchester and Ashton, but owing to the demand for silk hats instead of beavers, the occupation is now at a low ebb, and hundreds to whom it once afforded subsistence have enlisted in the army. We went from the old hand-loom weaver's to the house of a man who had been a beaver hatter, but who now gained his bread by winding silk for the construction of the new style of hats. The house was in a muddy lane, half the dwellings of which were ruinous and uninhabited. We found the husband presiding at a winding apparatus, which his son, a boy of five years of age, turned. The room in which the machine was bestowed, opened from the kitchen and sitting chamber. The aspect of things here was much brighter than at the last house. The man used to earn at his old trade 5s. or 6s. a day. He now earned, one week with another, 12s. Some days he made 3s., some days 2s., but he had often to "clem"[1] for want of work. However, as I have said, his average earnings were 12s. a week. It is his house I wish principally to notice. It was a sort of compromise between a house, properly so called, and a cellar. The lane without was undrained and unpaved, and the mud lay more than ankle deep all along it. From this vile thoroughfare you entered the house by a door, certainly not two feet in width, and down a high step, which brought the stone-flagged floor a good eighteen inches beneath the level of the lane. The consequence was, that the place was reeking with damp. There was tolerably decent furniture, a clock and other little matters; but the air of both the rooms had that wet earthy smell peculiar to underground places – and the moisture welling up marked with obvious stains the outlines of the flagstones which formed the floor. For this house this occupant paid £5 a year. It was an unwholesome place, he said, but he could not get sufficiently beforehand with the world to move to a better. The wife told me that she had never had a day's health since they lived there. Nothing

---

[1] "Clem" to starve with hunger.

but coughs and colds that she could not get rid of, and asthma settling on her chest. The poor woman was evidently in a critical pulmonary state. The wet cold air was killing her.

There are very few weavers out of work at Ashton, but I desired my guide to take me to the house of one. It was situated – I am still talking about the old part of Ashton – in a sort of broad *cul-de-sac*, so broad that it might almost be called a square. There may have been altogether thirty or forty houses composing it; and near one end of the open square was situated a great ash-pit and three or four privies, common to all the inhabitants, and ingeniously placed so as to be by far the most conspicuous objects in the place. In the low room of the house which we entered, two men, father and son, one of them in the prime of life, the other perhaps between sixty and seventy, were seated on either side of the hearth, listlessly peeling potatoes. On a small table beside them were the remains of breakfast – a coffee-pot, a dirty cup or two, and a filthy pewter spoon. The younger man had been sixteen weeks out of work. He looked wretchedly ill and languid; indeed, as he said, he had never been well since he was "down with the cholera". His wife was working in the mill. She earned about 9s. a week. He had been flung out of work owing to his having refused to submit to what he considered an unjust abatement of 5s. There was nothing absolutely squalid in the appearance of the room. Its worst feature was the listless, soddened look of the two men as they pursued their unfitting household toil. The old man had 2s. a week from the union, and went errands, or did any such odd job as he could obtain. The family amounted in all to seven.

At the dinner hour, in a cotton town, you have always ample opportunity for catching the general characteristics of the appearance of the population. "You can take stock of the workpeople," as a millowner phrased it to me, when they come flocking out of the factories. The appearance of the Ashton operatives is, I think, on the whole, superior to that of their Manchester brethren, and more akin to that of the population of the country mills. It may have been that my visit being on a Monday had something to do with the matter; but certainly the operatives, especially the women and girls, looked very much cleaner, both in skin and clothes, than the spinners and weavers of Manchester. Most of the girls wore necklaces of some sort – generally imitation coral, and both men and boys almost universally rejoiced in a species of round white felt hats, in Manchester called "wide awakes", and here dignified by the curious title of "bobbin nudgers".

The system of the millowners building and letting out comfortable cottages to their workpeople prevails as much, or even more in Ashton than in any town in Lancashire. It is common, particularly in the outskirts, to see every mill surrounded with neat streets of perfectly uniform dwellings, clean and cheerful in appearance and occupied by the "hands". The first of these snug little colonies to which we went was that attached to the mills of Messrs. Buckley.[1] Here are ranged in rows and squares, some of them with gardens attached, a little town of dwellings, regularly planned, and each house let, according to the number of rooms which it contains, at 3s., 3s. 9d., and 4s. 6d. If a garden be attached, a few shillings annually are charged in addition. The Messrs.

---

[1] At Ryecroft. Ryecroft Place, in Ryecroft Street, is a row of 16 houses with small front gardens and is dated 1838.

Buckley, I am informed, live among their people, and are in the habit of familiar intercourse with them – facts which operate as very great checks upon drunkenness and all sorts of disorderly behaviour. "If a master," says Mr Tipping, "never puts eyes on a man from Saturday till Monday, he may be drunk all that time with impunity; but here any conduct of the kind can't fail to be noticed, and so the man at once gets a hint that if he doesn't mend his manners he may look out for other employment. Such a thing as an application for parish relief from the people hereabouts," Mr Tipping added, "is scarcely ever heard of." The cottage gardens were, when I visited them, one and all fluttering with linen drying upon lines and hedges.

We afterwards proceeded to visit a street of cottages, erected by Messrs. Kershaw,[1] for their people. The outer doors led at once into the sitting rooms – a style of building which I was sorry to see persevered in. Otherwise the houses were all that could be desired. The floors were paved, with flag stones, but perfectly free from moisture, and generally sprinkled with white glistening sand. In each there was a parlour, a kitchen opening from it, and a yard and proper conveniences behind. The kitchen grate was furnished with a good range, including an oven and an ample boiler; and water from a neighbouring spring was laid on, with a sink and all its due apparatus. There were two bed-rooms upstairs. For a house of this kind 3s. 6d. per week was charged. The rent used to be 3s., the tenants paying the local rates; but the change has lately been made with their full concurrence. In the first house which I entered I found a respectable looking woman, a widow. She was

---

[1] At Guide Bridge

peeling potatoes for dinner. Two of her sons worked in the mill – one was a spinner, the other a piecer under him. The first earned 25s., the second 7s., a week. In many of the houses in this row, I was very glad to perceive an apparatus for converting yarn into hank, which was worked by the wife at home. A good hand could, I was informed, make 10s. a week at this process, and I was assured that a woman could easily earn 4s., and have, at the same time, ample leisure for attending to her household duties and taking care of her children.

The last mill cottages which I visited were those built by the Messrs. Mason and Sons.[1] The first thing which these gentlemen did, in laying out the ground, was to spend £1,000 in drainage, by which the refuse from every house is carried down into the river. The cottages are of two kinds – four and six roomed. For the former, 3s. per week is charged; for the latter 4s. 3d. per week. The inhabitants of the better class of houses are, therefore, voters. I inspected one of the four-roomed class. There was a lobby, and the stairs leading to the bedrooms were nicely carpeted. The front room was furnished strictly as a parlour; but the back one, or kitchen, which opened into a flagged yard, was obviously the ordinary sitting room.

I went over two mills in Ashton – one, working ten hours, that of the Messrs. Redfern;[2] the other working twelve, that of the Messrs. Mason and Sons. In both of these factories I was encouraged to examine the people upon any points I pleased. The manager at Messrs. Redfern's factory told me that one of the women, whom I had at random selected for examination from

---

[1] The Oxford "colony," close to the Masons' first Oxford Mill, built in 1845.

[2] John Redfern and Sons, Bank Field Mills.

the weaving shed, was worth more than £100. At the Messrs. Mason's I was furnished with a note of the wages weekly paid to the different classes of spinners in their employment, giving an average of more than £2 2s. to each spinner, and a general average for adults, in all the branches of the employment, including skilled and unskilled labour, of £1 2s. 5d. It must be distinctly observed, however, that piecers are not included in the calculation. The Messrs. Mason work twelve hours, but employ no relays of children or women. They find it quite practicable to carry on the business of a great cotton-spinning establishment for two hours a day with the help only of adult males – a fact to which it is important that its due weight should be attached.

I have before alluded to the sporting propensities of the handloom weavers. I learn that, in better times, the same spirit actuated the cotton, flax, and woollen hand-loom weavers of Ashton. There is, or used to be, a capital pack of harriers kept in the vicinity, and the Ashton weavers, armed with huge leaping-sticks by the help of which they could take hedges and ditches as well as the boldest rider of the hunt, were usual attendants on the pack. The mill system has, however, utterly extirpated every vestige of the ancient sporting spirit. The regularity of hours and discipline preserved seem, by rendering any such escapades out of the question, to have at length obliterated everything like a desire for, or idea of, them. The taste for botany, common to the district, seems, however, nearly as strong in Ashton as in Manchester. I observed a public-house kept by an enthusiast in the science, called the "Botanical Tavern."

OLDHAM

THE VISITOR to Oldham will find it essentially a mean-looking straggling town, built upon both sides and crowning the ridge of one of the outlying spurs which branch from the neighbouring "back-bone of England". The whole place has a shabby underdone look. The general appearance of the operatives' houses is filthy and smouldering. Airless little back streets and close nasty courts are common; pieces of dismal waste ground – all covered with wreaths of mud and piles of blackened brick and rubbish – separate the mills, which are often of small dimensions and confined and crowded appearance. The shops cannot be complimented, the few hotels are no better than taverns, and altogether the place, to borrow a musical simile, seems far under concert pitch. I observed, as I walked up from the railway station, melancholy clusters of gaunt, dirty, unshorn men, lounging on the pavement. These, I heard, were principally hatters, a vast number of whom are out of employment. Another feature of the place was the quantity of dogs of all kinds which abounded – dog-races and dogfights being both common among the lowest orders of the inhabitants.

The union of Oldham includes eight townships, and comprises a population of about 85,000 souls, 50,000 of whom actually live in the town itself. The operations of the union only commenced in 1847. During that year as much as £262 was spent in out-door relief in a week. The amount at present paid is about £112 per week for out-door relief, and there are about 450 paupers in the workhouse, which is, however, very inadequate to the wants of the population. The union is often obliged to pay for beds at common lodging-houses, for the vagrants and destitute tramps whom they cannot take into the house. The acreage of the union is 11,000, and, like the neighbouring district of Ashton, it has escaped with about thirty fatal cases of cholera.

Oldham from Glodwick, 1860

I shall give an account of the operatives of Oldham, in so far as they seem to differ from the average cotton population of Manchester and the surrounding towns. In Oldham, there are a great number of small capitalists renting floors or small portions of factories. These employers have themselves generally risen from the mule or the loom and maintain in a great degree their operative appearance, thoughts, and habits. Many of the coarser operations performed upon the coarsest sorts of cotton are carried on – numerous mills are "spinning waste" as it is called – that is, working up for the commonest purposes the material rejected as refuse by the factories engaged in producing the finer and medium degrees of goods. The stuff subjected to the operation of these Oldham mills, immortalized by Mr.

Ferrand[1] as "Shoddy" and "Devil's dust," is specially produced in its manufacture. Those helots called the "Low Irish" are to be found in considerable numbers at Oldham, and I shall shortly describe their homes and haunts.

One of my first cares was to ascertain, so far as I could, the difference in the tone of relationship subsisting between the class of operative capitalists in Oldham and the workpeople, as compared with that existing between the mill hands and the larger and more assuming capitalists of greater towns. This is exactly one of those delicate social points with reference to which the passing visitor is compelled to seek for information at second hand. The particulars which I received from the different sources to which I applied differed widely. By two or three intelligent persons, life-long residents in Oldham, I was assured that the class of operative-employers were by far the most popular with the mill hands. "These masters," I was informed, "are just the same as if they were the fellow workman of those they employ. They dress much in the same way, they live much in the same way, their habits and language are almost identical, and when they 'get on the spree' they go and drink and sing in low taverns with their own working hands." I inquired in what sort of houses these masters lived? "In houses a little better and larger than the common dwellings, but managed inside very much in the same way."

"Do they educate their sons as gentlemen?" "They seldom do. They may give them a better education than

---

[1] William Busfield Ferrand (1809-1889), the factory reformer. He was Tory M.P. for Knaresborough from 1841-47 and became known as "The Working Man's Friend" as a result of his attacks on factory conditions.

the sons of common men; but they wish them to supply their own places, and to be just like what they themselves are." My informants added that although masters and men often caroused together, yet, on occasions of difference arising between them, the masters would get dreadfully abusive, and terribly bad blood would ensue. This latter piece of information, as well as a little experience of human nature, inclined me rather to credit the opposite view, urged among others by Mr. Clegg, the courteous clerk to the union, that the larger capitalists, the men who had not themselves been operatives in the memory of the existing generation, were the class of millowners most generally and most continuously popular:

"Their establishments are the larger and the better regulated. The work there is more regular, the rooms often better ventilated and more pleasant, and all sorts of minor conveniences for washing, shifting clothes, &c., better ordered than in the smaller mills."

Oldham is tolerably well supplied with water, by means of pipes from the adjoining hills. Most of the springs in the town have been dried up by the coalmines hitting the same strata as those in which the water runs. The pit population are generally reckoned inferior, morally and intellectually, to the mill population. The wages of the former have materially suffered from the Ten Hours Bill, the factory engines not requiring the same amount of fuel. The wages earned by a good pitman at present cannot exceed, if it amounts to, a guinea a week. In this district the women never work, and never have worked, in the collieries.

Under the guidance of two intelligent relieving officers, I set out to see some of the characteristic manufacturers and some of the characteristic population of the place. It was about noon, and the people were pouring out from the mills on their way home to dinner. I observed that the women almost universally wore silk bandanna handkerchiefs fluttering round their heads. "It has always been so in Oldham," I was informed. "They would pinch hard rather than go with a plain cap instead of a silk handkerchief." Presently I overtook two little girls, the eldest not above eight years of age, each carrying a baby some three or four months old in a pick-a-back fashion, the infant being snugly enough wrapped up, and only its head protruding from beneath the cloak of its bearer. These girls, I was informed, were nurses, paid for taking charge of the children while their mothers laboured in the mills. I accosted them.

"So, you have these children to nurse! What do the mothers pay you?"

"Oh, please sir, they pay us 1s. 6d. a week for each baby."

"And where are you taking them now?"

"Oh, please sir, to their mothers. They come out of the mills now, and we carry the babies down to meet them, and the mothers give them suck, when they're at dinner."

"And do you take the babies in the morning, and nurse them all day till dinner-time, and then take them to their mothers, and then fetch them back, and at last take them home at night?"

"Yes, sir, that's what we do; but sometimes, you know, the babies have little sisters, as old as us, and then they are nursed at home."

The first manufacturing process which we saw was the cleaning of "shoddy." Unlike any stage of the preparation of cotton which I had seen, this was carried on in an isolated building, situated in the midst of a piece of doleful-looking waste ground. There was a small steam-engine at one extremity, which turned five or six "devils," or coarse and primitive-looking blowing machines, each being placed in a compartment of its own, somewhat like the stall of a stable, and attended by a single guardian, whose business it was to feed the machine with handfuls of the coarse dirty cotton. The door was in each case open, or the dust and flying fibres from the machine would have rendered the air unbreathable. As it was, I could not but pity the gaunt-looking men who tended the devils. I questioned them, but they seemed loath to complain, admitting, however, that the flying "dust and stuff" gave them pains in the chest and terribly hacking coughs and asthma. One of them only remarked, "We don't get old men, sir, at this work." They were paid from 8s. to 12s. per week. The refuse of each devil was consigned to the next coarser machine. The products of the better sort of machines are wrought up into quilts and coarse sheeting; those of the next coarser kind are worked into a coarse paper; from those of the third coarser kind are spun candlewicks; the product of the lowest sort of devils is the material with which flock beds are stuffed; and the refuse from these, heaps of oily seeds and broken and tangled fibres, inseparably mashed up with dirt, is sold for manure. Each shed or stall in this concern was let out for £25 a year, the landlord finding the motive power. The engine spun ceaselessly on; and the asthmatic labourers, each in his stall, between a heap of impure cotton and the whirling devil, pursued amid the dense and fibre laden air, his monotonous and unwholesome toil.

From thence we went to visit two factories, in one of which are spun very coarse threads, intended for the Indian market, and in the other of which are manufactured candlewicks. The proprietors of both politely accompanied me in my rounds. They had been working men, and were, in language, manner, and dress, very much akin to the people they employed. In the coarse spinning mill – a small airless building – I found an apparently chronic system of dirt and neglect prevailing. The stairs were rickety and filth-encrusted, and the drawing and spinning rooms not only hot, but what is much worse, chokey, and stifling, and reeking with oil. The women employed exhibited, in a palpably exaggerated degree, the unwholesome characteristics of the appearance of the Manchester mill-workers. They were not so much sallow or pale, as absolutely yellow, and their leanness amounted to something unpleasant to look at. The mill was of the old construction, and had no means of ventilation. The wages of the people ranged a shilling or two beneath the average of the medium Manchester rate.

From this place I had but a few paces to walk, partially through narrow courts and by a rickety, wooden bridge over a green pool of stagnant water, to the mill where candlewicks were manufactured. The establishment consisted of but a single room, not more than six feet high. Here the cotton refuse used was cleaned, drawn, and spun. The heat, the stink, the flying dust were almost overpowering. At one end of the room stood a blowing machine of the rudest construction, and the mules and drawing frames were built to correspond. The boy who principally attended the "devil" was covered from head to foot with the clinging fibres of floating wool. I exaggerate not one jot on the contrary, I use the metaphor simply to describe the fact when I say that the outline of his figure was clothed as it were with a halo of downy tissue. From this the state of the atmosphere may be imagined. The labour of the piecers was the most severe I have yet seen. The coarse knotty threads were continually breaking, and the attendants were therefore eternally hurrying about re-uniting them. The different pieces of mechanism were so very closely crammed that it was difficult to walk between them, without the risk of being injured by the unboxed wheels and cranks which worked around. The floor was soppy with the rankest oil; the small windows were almost obscured by coatings of woolly fibre which clung to the interior of the casements, as snow sometimes does to the exterior of panes and sashes; and the bare joists and rafters were furred with the same downy-like substance, as stakes set in the sea are clothed with clustering weeds. Altogether the place was unfitted for human beings to work or breathe in. When you looked through the beams, the flying straps, and revolving wheels, you saw the toiling slatternly workpeople as through a fog of fibry dust and floating cotton particles. I asked the principal spinner which he preferred, the Ten Hours Bill or the twelve, and he gave his vote unhesitatingly for the latter: "Couldn't afford to do with ten hours wages." The mill however, if I remember right, only works ten hours a day. The wages of the spinners ranged from 9s. to 11s. per week.

I afterwards went over two small mills, compartments of which are rented by different individuals. Both were dirty, and constructed in the old-fashioned unventilated style. The workpeople looked more gaunt, yellow, and slatternly than they are in the average of factories; but I saw nothing calling for any special notice, over and above what I have said of the coarse spinning mill already alluded to. The candlewick making establishment was, out of all sight, the most repulsive working place I have seen in Lancashire.

Understanding that here and there, scattered in cellars or perched in garrets, were a few old men who still wove cotton by the handloom, I requested to be introduced to one of the practitioners of this fast-expiring trade. We accordingly descended a narrow flight of area steps, leading beneath the surface of a mean back street, and discovered two stone-paved rooms, dark and squalid; one of which served for the common apartment; the other, a mere closet, was almost entirely occupied by one of the old-fashioned treddle looms. In the first room was some coarse deal furniture, and one of those low broad beds raised about a foot above the floor and covered with truckle, which by their shape generally appear intended for accommodating at a pinch perhaps four persons. Two dirty children were lying fighting and squalling upon the floor. The woman of the house was a sturdy dame of some sixty years. The man, who was at his work, had a gaunt, skeleton-like face and head, and thin white hair. By way of beginning the conversation, I remarked that the "pegging-stick" which he had just laid down – that is, the stick used to jerk the shuttle was beautifully constructed. I had never seen such another. It was fluted and wreathed, exactly suiting the grasp of the fingers and thumb. "Constructed!" said the weaver – "constructed, indeed! Why, man, I did that myself. I wore them hollow bits in the hard wood with my own flesh, in the long working days of fifteen years. Aye, I loved to weave better nor to play in the road. I've not been an idle man, sir."

I asked what he paid for his rooms. The rent of the two was 1s. 9d. a week. What were his wages ? He was old, and soom'mut failed now, and with his wife to wind for him, he could only get 1s. work as hard as he might. They had parish assistance, however; and, besides, his daughter worked at factory. Those were her children I had seen in the other room.

"By the way," said one of my companions to the old woman, who had joined us, "Has your daughter affiliated that last child of hers yet ?" The parents did not think she had.

"So the children are illegitimate!" I observed.

"Yes," said their grandmother. "You see they're by different fathers, and she (the daughter) don't know which she would be happiest wi', and so she don't marry neyther."

The old man took the opportunity of observing quietly that, for himself, he did not trouble his head about them things, and that young people would be young people. Very soon after these naive declarations, both the old people began to boast of the excellence of their bringing up, and their regular attendance at church. I inquired into their domestic arrangements more particularly. The daughter fed herself and her two children, and paid her parents some trifling sum a week for lodging and attending to the children while she was at the mill. I tried to get at the literal particulars, but there were so many charges and counter charges, and deductions and sets off, of pennies and two-pences, that I gave up the financial part of the business in despair. They seldom or never saw meat, but lived on oat-cake, potatoes, porridge, and a little coffee. A pitcher of dark-looking liquid, which stood upon the table by the loom, held treacle beer, a sickly tasting stuff. The man said that even if he could get meat. his stomach was so feeble he could not digest it. He lived upon slops. His trade, he began to tell me, was a thriving one in his young days. "When old George III was king,[1] he could make £2 2s. a week easy. Twenty years ago he could make 20s. Now, without the parish, he would starve. He thought that altogether the people who worked in factories made nearly as much, taking them in families, as they could have done in the old time before the power-loom. But they spent the money in drink, instead of laying it by. They went much too often to the 'hush houses' (low beer-shops, frequently unlicensed). Also the young men had pigeon matches and dog fights, and gambling and drinking on the Lord's-day. indeed, last Sabbath morn he had been awakened by the whole family in the next cellar fighting together." I had some difficulty in getting a reply to the question – whether the working people altogether lived upon as good food and had as much of it as when he was a boy? At length he said, after much pondering, that he thought the people now-a-days "lived full as well."

From the old weaver's cellar, we went to visit some similar dwellings, situated in a group of close undrained and unpaved courts. These were occupied almost entirely by elderly women, who made precarious livings as laundresses. Several of these cellars, though miserably poor, were kept beautifully clean, and the little ornaments and paltry pictures ranged about the walls often showed a touching struggle between pinching poverty and a decent desire to keep up appearances. One cellar was, however, of a different

---

[1] 1760-1820.

stamp. We approached it along a foul subterraneous passage, and, on opening the door, a stench so abominable burst forth, that even my companions, accustomed to scenes of want and filth, recoiled, and called to the people in the room to open the single swinging pane in a window of about six – each pane being about four inches by three – looking out into a sort of slit rather than pit, dug down to the level of the window sill from a back court. The place was almost dark. It contained three low beds, covered with ragged, unmade wisps of bed clothes. A woman and a little girl sat upon stools cowering over a morsel of fire, and drinking tea, or some decoction which passed as such. In one of the beds lay a third female, moaning in her confinement. She was a married woman; her husband had left her, and she was now brought to bed of a child by another man. This woman was a mill worker. All the occupants of the room professed themselves unconscious of any smell whatever; but one of them having gone out for a moment, admitted on her return that the sewer was "rather bad to-day." It turned out that a drain, passing from some other part of the town, ran underneath the house, the stone flags were here and there broken, and through the slimy soil beneath, the foetid gases rose bubbling up, in such strength as to render it physically impossible for me to draw breath in the apartment. Yet the inmates had every aperture through which the fresh air could come carefully stopped, and complained when the door and window, or rather pane, was opened of the cold. The rent paid for these cellars is from 1s. to 1s. 9d, a week.

Our next visit was to the "low Irish" *quartier*. We first entered a kitchen, where a haggard man and woman were seated at tea. Above, the relieving officer told me, was an old man dying upon bundles of rags on the floor. He would not consent to be carried to the workhouse, and so he had 2s. a week where he was. Upon the floor of the kitchen were ranged a number of nicely tied brooms or brushes, made of fresh-smelling furze, or, as the people here called it, "ling" which grows in abundance on the neighbouring hills, and the cutting and forming of which into besoms constitutes almost the only work of the Irish adult population of Oldham. The man before us had, however, been a mill worker, but his chest could not stand the flying cotton dust, so he had to take to besom-making instead. It occupied him, he said, one day to go to the hill, cut the ling, and carry it home; another day to make the besoms, and the rest of the week was taken up, with the assistance of three of his children, in hawking them about for sale. A dozen fetched half-a-crown once, but the price was much lower – not one-half that now – so that in good weeks he could only make about four shillings. Two of his children worked in a factory, which helped them on a little. The worst was, however, that, as he heard, they were to be prevented from cutting ling because of destroying the cover for the grouse. What would become of him, if it was so, God only knew. The bread which he and his wife were eating, and upon which they chiefly lived, was made of oatmeal, baked soft, like the cakes called "barley scones" in Scotland, and of heavy and doughy texture.

At another house, occupied by an Irish family, which was filled with the sharp pungent smoke of the refuse ling used for firewood, a man, grimy, unshaven, and half clad, and yet who had in his face and proportions the making of a model stalwart Irish peasant, recapitulated the sad rumour that the ling cutting was to be stopped. He had to walk eight and a half miles for the ling, and carry home as much as he could on his back. One of the cutters "got a month (a month's imprisonment) the other day. Oh, begarra! but it was hard on the poor the gentry was." This man had been fifteen years residing in Oldham. He came from County Sligo.

We now proceeded to visit one of the Irish lodging-houses. A description of one will nearly serve for all. In the low kitchen, amid some wretched rickety furniture, and pots, pans, and broken plates, was littered huge heaps of the ling, among which lay sprawling, as they bound it into shape, three or four strapping young men, talking Irish to each other, and to the wretched drabs of ragged women who were cowering by the fireplace. In this room were two beds. In a back room. a similar manufactory was going on, and in it, among all sorts of wretched household litter – broken tubs, cracked jars, and pots full of all manner of filthy slops – was another bed – merely a bundle of rags shaken down upon a substratum of the all-pervading ling. There was a back yard, with an ashpit reeking of abominations. Up stairs were two little rooms. In one were three or four beds; in the other and larger, six. I examined the sheets; They were drab colour with unmitigated filth. The beds were made up on crazy bedsteads, fastened together with knotted ropes, and sometimes propped with big stones. The bed-posts, broken of different heights, sloped hither and thither. It was late in the day, but the beds had not been made – I question whether they ever are – nor the slops emptied. Sixpence a bed was the nominal price per night; so that three tramps could, as they often do, sleep together for twopence each; but the price varies with the influx of lodgers, sometimes sinking to a penny, to a halfpenny, indeed to anything which the poor creatures have. In the lower room was a daub of an oil painting in four compartments, representing four events in the career of a criminal the robbery, the apprehension, the trial, and the execution. Near it were paltry prints of the Virgin, and of saints exhibiting burning hearts; and beside them was a sort of allegorical chart, called "A Railway to Heaven, with a tunnel through Mount Calvary." The lodgers were nearly all hawkers of besoms. The men I had seen working in the house would be next day miles off, upon Saddleworth, gathering fresh material. Sometimes more than thirty people, men and women, slept in the three rooms which I have described. We went over more than a dozen of similar places – some a little better, some a little worse, than I have described. The owner of each house was always anxious to explain that half of the people we saw in the low rooms, cowering round the fire, wretched sodden-like men and women, were not lodgers, but merely "Naybours, sure, that comes in to see yez"; and usually upon our descent from the bedrooms the kitchen would be all but cleared of its occupants.

The poor-law authorities of Oldham are making exertions to improve the sanitary state of the worst districts of the town, but the Irish puzzle them excessively. "No sooner," I was informed "no sooner do we try to make the houses a little decent and wholesome, than the people leave them, and flock to other localities, to be driven thence with a like result." Fever – the "Irish fever" – that is, the most malignant species of spotted typhus, frequently breaks out. A very promising young medical man was swept away by it in Oldham a short time ago; and if the people resident in the dens I have described have, comparatively speaking, escaped the cholera, most certainly they owe more to their luck than their management.

"A court for King Cholera", Punch 1852

MACCLESFIELD

I AM writing at a window commanding the crowded market-place of a quaint, old-fashioned town. The houses are irregular and massed together in picturesque clumps, their outline serrated by crazy chimney-stacks and high-peaked gables. Opposite to me is an old buttressed Norman church – a gilt crown placed loyally above the weather cock, and a gilt mitre placed religiously above the crown. The market-place is built on top of a hill – steep lanes slope down from it in all directions, and through their openings you catch pleasant glimpses of distant healthy hills. A majority of the crowded shops display in their windows richest silks of the gayest patterns – gown-pieces, waistcoat-pieces and handkerchiefs of all hues and sizes. The market is crowded with stalls and booths and tents, and these are surrounded by chaffering customers. The wares displayed are here and there peculiar. Amid great heaps of vegetables and fruit, piled in pyramids upon the pavement, are the stalls of the vendors of blacking – for here is manufactured the material which polishes the boots and shoes of a great part of Lancashire. One family make and sell near half a ton weekly. Close to the blacking merchant is a quack, with his portable furnaces and retorts, distilling his remedies before a gaping crowd of onlookers. Next to him sits, in his canvas-roofed tent, a bread merchant – home baked wheaten loaves on one side of his shop – round doughy cakes of oatmeal, sold at a penny a-piece, piled up on the other. Hard by is a stall filled with hares, rabbits, black game and plovers; and just before it stands a man with a huge inverted umbrella filled with coarsely-made brown stays. The aspect of the people is on the whole comfortable, and well-to-do. The vendors are generally country folks, burly farmers, or knowing pedlars. The buyers are the people of the town, among whom the lower class of females appear decidedly better dressed and better looking than the factory women. Nevertheless, most of them do work in the mills. A short turn through the old fashioned town, with its narrow streets and its ranges of stairs from one elevated plateau to another, will reveal many factories, similar in appearance to the cotton mills, but smaller in size, and crowned with chimneys, which, though tall, are not yet so tall as most of those with which we have been lately dealing.

These are silk mills; the population is a population of silk throwsters and weavers; for I have been describing the principal features of the market-place and the market-day in Macclesfield, the capital of the silk trade in England.

Macclesfield is situated among the Cheshire hills. The population of the township was, at the last census, 56,035, and it has since increased, but by no means rapidly. The number of persons in the receipt of parish relief, on the 1st of January, 1848, was 2,974. The value of life in Macclesfield is about 1 in 38 – a proportion similar to that of the majority of the smaller cotton towns. The number of marriages in 1846, according to the rites of the church, was 532; otherwise, 42. Of the 1,148 persons thus united, 350 women and 178 men, making a total of 528 persons, or rather under 50 per cent., signed with their marks. Of the persons in question, 115 women, or nearly 20 per cent., were under age, and 46 men. The legitimate births during 1846 were 2,223, and the illegitimate 238 – the proportion being about one to eight. Out of 825 deaths, 214 were those of persons under one year of age

– a proportion very much smaller than the average of the cotton towns. These broad facts afford landmarks in making our first advances towards estimating the condition of the Macclesfield silk manufacturing population. It is a population increasing in a much slower ratio than that of the cotton towns. Thus the female inhabitants of the neighbouring township of Stockport rose between 1831 and 1841 from 36,000 to 44,000, while those of Macclesfield increased only from 25,000 to 28,000.

A young girl winding pirns at Hall's Mill. See p. v.

The manufacture of silk may be said to be the only one in Macclesfield. There is but a single cotton mill in the town. Silk has been the staple of the place for more than half a century. Before that time Macclesfield was but a paltry village. "We took the trade," said a manufacturer to me, "from Spitalfields, and now the country places about are taking it from us; and with every successive stage of the expansion of the manufacture the wages seem to come down." About one half of the labouring population of Macclesfield work at home, and the other half in the mills. The home labourers are exclusively weavers; the mill labourers are principally engaged in throwing, doubling and other processes, analogous, in a certain degree, to the drawing and spinning of cotton mills – in preparing the threads which are intertwisted by the loom. By far the largest proportion of the mill population is female, the weavers who work looms in the mills being inconsiderable in number, compared with those who work at home. I may add that the amount of silk thread spun in Macclesfield is much greater than the amount woven there. The warp and the shute,[1] being prepared for the loom, are sent out all over the silk weaving districts of Lancashire and Cheshire for the process to be completed. The wages earned in and out of the mills in Macclesfield do not materially vary. The throwsters and spinners in the mills have the most regular work. The weavers can earn higher wages when in employment, but their looms stand idle upon the average fully three months in the year. A weaver may, one season with another, make from 10s. to 12s. a week; a female throwster or doubler in the mill from 8s. to 9s. The rate of wages, hours of work, species of employment and other particulars will, however, be best understood from the following details of the different branches of the silk trade, gathered from

---

[1] "Shute – the thread carried across the warp by the shuttle.

personal observation of every department and of every process, and from the personally collected testimony of the workpeople.

I have said that the silk mills are generally smaller than the cotton factories. They are also generally cleaner and filled with a purer atmosphere. There is no necessity for keeping the temperature of any of the rooms above 50 degrees; and nothing analogous to, or resembling, the flying dust and floating film which abound in certain stages of the cotton manufacture is to be found. The machinery of a silk mill is altogether simpler, slower, and less overwhelming in its power and vastness than that which spins thread from the cotton wool. The work is cleaner, too, and, in many respects, is well fitted for females, who are enabled to dress with far more neatness and propriety than the girls in the cotton factories. In several of the silk mills which I have gone over, the girls were dressed rather in the style of milliners' apprentices than of ordinary female operatives; and if good looks may be taken as a test of satisfactory physical condition, I have no hesitation in saying that the general physical condition of the young women employed in throwing and winding silk is excellent. Very few married women work in the silk mills – the quantity of labour to be performed at home being so considerable that a natural and generally understood arrangement comes almost insensibly into force, and tends to keep within their own dwellings those whose absence from them would be most undesirable and domestically unprofitable. The Ten Hours Bill applies to silk factories, with certain modifications as to infant labour – a child being there accounted "a young person" at eleven years of age, instead of thirteen – a concession made by the Legislature on account of the healthier and cleaner species of employment carried on in the silk mills. What that employment is I shall now shortly describe.

There are in the silk mills no operations analogous to the cleaning and carding of cotton. The first stages of the manufacture have, so to speak, been already performed by the worm which spins the cocoon. The raw fibres of silk are imported from France, Italy or China in compact bundles, which are sorted and arranged according to the fineness and quality of the material, by women. The labour thus employed is, of course, physically very light, but the post is one of some responsibility, and demanding considerable acquaintance with the varying qualities of the silk. The wages paid to the sorters may be stated at 10s. a week. The silk is next plunged into hot water – the operation being generally managed by men, who are also employed in different odd jobs about the mill, and who may make from 15s. to 20s. a week. After this purification comes the first process of manufacture. It is the simple one of transferring the thread from the circular pieces of framework, upon which the sorter has put it, to bobbins. The winding is effected, of course, by steam power, the bobbins and wheels being arranged upon long frames, attended by women and girls. Each woman has the charge of four and a half of these frames, and she has an assistant girl under her. The work consists principally in shifting the wheels and bobbins when they respectively get empty and full, and in re-uniting the fibres which may chance to break. The dunter, as the principal operative is called, gets about 7s. 6d. per week, and the little girl, her assistant, from 5s. 6d. to 6s. The temperature in these winding-rooms is generally agreeable, and, as I have said, the appearance of the females is prepossessing. Although their wages are so decidedly lower than those paid in the cotton mills, the silk girls seem to belong to altogether a superior and more refined class of society than the female cotton workers – an appearance to be accounted for by the cleaner and more wholesome nature of their work. In several of the rooms which I visited, the girls' bonnets and shawls were neatly arranged along the walls; the machinery worked almost noiselessly, and there was a curious absence of the clatter and systematic hurry-skurry which marks the interior of a cotton mill.

The next process is that of cleaning. Here we have a similar system of frames and female attendants, the latter being, however, almost entirely girls. The silk is wound from one bobbin to another, passing through an implement very like an all but closed pair of scissors, which clears away all sorts of extraneous dirt and filaments. The labour of the girls is purely of a superior tending species, their charge being to renew the broken threads, and to keep a due supply of bobbins. The wages earned are from 6s. to 6s. 3d. per week. It will be seen that the work extracted from both these classes of females is exceedingly light and simple. Still, as in the cotton processes, they require to be continually upon their legs. The thread is next carried to the doublers. The term explains the nature of the operation, which is in a certain degree analogous to the drawing process in cotton manufacture. The superintendents of the frames are still young women; and their work requiring more attention and more skill than those demanded by the inferior operations, their wages average 7s. 6d. The thread is now ready for being spun or, to speak more correctly, twisted – an operation known as throwing. The apparatus used for this process differs materially from the cotton mule, having no backward or forward motion. Each machine is a compact series of spindles, bobbins and wheels, ranged one above the other, so as to necessitate the spinner or throwster availing himself of a triangularly-built ladder, placed upon small wheels, in order to enable him to superintend the working of the higher ranges of spindles. The motion of these is excessively quick, making in many instances, not less than 3,000 revolutions in a minute. The spinner, in attending to the lower tiers, has a good deal of unpleasant stooping work to perform, and the atmosphere of the room has, generally speaking, a sickly oily odour. Each spinner is attended by a boy, who pieces, as in the cotton mills. The men earn about 12s. a week – some a little more, some a little less – and the boys about 6s. 6d. All these estimates of wages are to be understood as applying to ten hours' daily work. The thread, having been spun, is now taken to the dyers, where it is tinted with the hue desired. On its being brought, back, a series of reeling and winding operations, very similar to those already described, is gone through. These are, as formerly, conducted by young women and girls, but their wages range higher than those of their predecessors, averaging from 7s. 6d. to 8s. per week. A number of purely technical processes – depending upon the sort of pattern which is to be woven – are gone through before the silk is finally ready for the loom. No description of these would be at all intelligible; but I may add that one of them, called "bear-warping", is the highest species of labour performed by women in silk mills, and brings them not less than 12s. per week. Another operation, called "coupling and knitting", also connected with the arrangement of the silk for the pattern-weaving looms, is conducted by women and little girls. The work here is light and little skilled, consisting principally of passing threads through the constellations of holes in the pattern cards, masses of which are to be seen hanging from the top of Jacquard looms.[1] The young women earn only 5s., and the little girls not above 3s. A superintendent, who also works, has 10s. per week.

We now pass to the weaving department. Very little silk, and that only of the coarsest kind, is woven by power. A small quantity of bandannas[2] are thus turned out in Macclesfield; but in the production of the higher class of silk fabrics, and in all fancy goods, the delicacy and intelligence of human labour is requisite, and the Jacquard is never beholden for its motion to the steam-engine. A silk weaving shed, filled with Jacquard looms, is a curious looking place, somewhat reminding one of a forest of apparently tangled rigging, so multitudinous are the upright and horizontal beams, and so perplexingly complicated are the threads, cards and strings, which stretch from one to the other. Most of the silk mills in Macclesfield weave as well as throw upon the establishment. Indeed, the masters discourage the domestic weaving, particularly with reference to the finer sorts of fancy goods. They wish to have the men more under their eye than the former would be at their homes; and they urge that they are much more sure of the work being turned out at the time appointed. The

---

[1] The Jacquard loom, so called because of the automatic punched card attachment invented by the French weaver Joseph Marie Jacquard (1752-1834). This made possible the weaving of intricate patterns and pictures. The first version of Jacquard's mechanism appeared in 1801 and was perfected during the following three years.
[2] Bandanna – a richly coloured yellow or white spotted handkerchief.

coarser sort of weaving is, however, almost universally performed away from the mill. I have visited Macclesfield at rather an unpropitious time for seeing the Jacquard weavers at their work – the winter fashions having been completed, and the labour upon those for the spring not yet commenced. In the large weaving shed of Messrs. Brodrick and Brinsley[1] only one or two Jacquards were in operation – the rest were waiting to be filled for the spring fashions.

A Jacquard weaver in full work, at a superior piece of goods, can still earn as much as 35s. a week; but taking the year round, including his seasons of enforced idleness, his wages, at least so far as Macclesfield goes, may be stated as averaging 10s. to 11s. In this estimation, masters and men very generally agreed. I enquired whether, in seasons of slackness of work, the weavers labouring in the mill had the preference in respect to what work there was. The answer was, "Decidedly not. In such times they all fare alike." Still several of the domestic weavers informed me that they thought that the men who worked in the mills had more regular employment than the home operatives. The former class have, at all events, rather higher wages, because they decidedly do obtain the greater proportion of superior work. I may add here, that the spinners or throwsters are generally young men, and that adult males are employed in this capacity in only a few of the mills. It is no uncommon thing for a throwster, when he grows up, to take to weaving, in which case he has to pay from £5 to £10 for being taught. These men have frequently a local reputation for their ingenuity in useful branches of

---

[1] Directories list the firm of Charles Brinsley, of Anderton Street. This was one of the two Macclesfield silk concerns to win a gold medal at the Great Exhibition of 1851.

160

minor mechanics, and about Macclesfield they are famed for making mousetraps and analogous pieces of domestic machinery.

From the mills I proceeded to inspect the habitations and workplaces of some of the domestic weavers. A street of medium appearance having been pointed out to me as being solely occupied by silk hand-loom weavers, I visited five of the houses, taking them at random. In each I was cordially received and readily furnished with all the information for which I asked. The houses inhabited by the Macclesfield hand-loom weavers are very generally similar in construction, having been mostly all built with an eye to the staple manufacture of the place. They consist, in nine cases out of ten, of five rooms: two on the ground floor, one serving as sitting-room and kitchen, and the other as a scullery. On the first floor are generally a couple of bed-rooms – those into which I peeped were clean and neat – and then, ascending a ladder and making your way through a trapdoor, you reach the loom-shop, which is always located in the garret, and which is exclusively devoted to the operation of weaving.

In the first house which I visited, the lower room was fitted up much in the same style as that which prevails in the medium class operatives' houses in Manchester. The eternal rocking chair stood by the fire; there were small prints hung upon the walls, mingling with shining pot lids, and placed around ranges of shelves filled with crockery and all sorts of minor household matters. One of the bed-rooms was furnished, the other was littered with portions of the apparatus of looms. The garret was a lofty and airy room, the roof rising in a sort of peak – it was a corner house – to the height of about ten feet. The window extended longitudinally, almost the whole length of the room. In the apartment there stood, I think, five treddle-looms and a Jacquard, and a young man and two girls were at work. The male weaver informed me that he was making silk for handkerchiefs. He was a journeyman, and he paid 5s. a week rent for the Jacquard at which he was seated. He paid this rent to the undertaker. The undertaker was the man who rented the whole house, to whom the looms belonged, and who also found work for the journeymen and apprentices. In short, the undertaker seemed to act as a sort of middleman between the weavers and the masters. The latter gave him the prepared silk, on his promising that it should be returned within a certain time woven – and then he in turn distributed the material to the workers, bargaining for the completion of the job by the stipulated period, but not interfering with the hours of labour, which, except in the case of apprentices, are at the option of the weaver. The undertaker sometimes worked, and sometimes contented himself with acting as a sort of agent. Very often he had a family who worked for him. If he had not, he took apprentices, and let out his rooms to journeymen. The weaver to whom I was speaking said that he could make, when in full work, 23s. a week, but that was only for the best species of weaving which he had to do. Besides, he was generally out of work altogether for about three months in the year. Striking an average, he thought he could earn about 10.s a week the year round. For this he generally worked twelve hours a day. Although the rent of a Jacquard was 5s., other looms could be rented for 3s. 6d. Apprentices generally served five years, and received one half of their earnings. This man was decidedly of opinion that machinery had done no harm to his trade. The second weaver whom I visited was unintelligent and gave little or no information. The third was an old man, and disposed to be frankly communicative. He believed that the Macclesfield silk weavers were better off than the generality in the country places – in Middleton for example, because in Macclesfield the better sort of fabrics were generally produced. He himself was making silk for handkerchiefs. He considered that the weaving of eight dozen a week was very fair work, and he was paid 2s. 1d. per dozen. He was thus earning rather less than 17s. per week. For this he toiled sometimes 12, sometimes 13 hours a day. He had work, he thought, for two-thirds of the year. Machinery, in his estimation, had greatly injured the trade. Why else was it that 30 years ago he could earn as much in one week as he could now do in three, working very hard, too? He thought, upon the average, that people worked twice as hard now as they did when he was a boy. The work was more "drierd" (more continuously difficult) than it was in the old time. People were more easily satisfied with silks then than now. At present they were hard to please. And everything went so much on fashion, and fashions changed so fast that it was difficult either for master or man to suit the market. The lowest sort of silk weaving was the manufacture of greys for bandanna handkerchiefs. The weavers were paid 5s. 1d. per cut for this sort of silk twenty years ago. Now they couldn't earn more than 2s. 6d., with harder work because the "shute" was finer and required greater care. The lowest amount of wages made by a weaver he put down as about 7s. 8d. to 8s. Working figured goods with the Jacquard, they could make a considerable deal of money, 24s. or 26s. a week; but the Jacquards were standing half the year. The man whose information I am recording was an undertaker, and his journeymen paid him 3s., 3s. 6d. and 5s. for loom rent. He went on to say that the frequently recurring periods of stagnation in trade kept the weavers poor during the time they had full work. They were busy sometimes, but they were poor always. Twenty years ago people lived better than now. They had plenty of substantial food, but at present, where one got it a dozen missed it. The people in the mills were better off, particularly the throwsters, than the people out of them, because the mill hands had more regular employment. It was the sudden changes in the taste for fancy articles that made the sudden fluctuations in the demand for goods, and occasioned a great deal of the poor weavers' poverty. Mayhap the master would give an order for a certain pattern. Well, all at once the taste would pass away, and the silks would lie upon the shelves. Soom'mut new was always coming up, and that made the changes from the busy times to the slack times. The trade was very uncertain – so uncertain that the masters were afraid to speculate so much as they would if they could sell their goods steadier, and therefore they gave small orders – great ones might be left upon their hands. He thought that, one with another, the weavers in the mill might earn 12s. or 14s. a week; working at home he would not put the average higher than 10s. a week. The house in which he lived had four rooms besides the loom-garret. He paid £10 a year rent for it besides taxes. It had good drains, and there was water laid on – all complete and handy.

On my way down stairs I looked into the different rooms and found things tidy and (in a homely way) comfortable. It was a Saturday – the weekly washing and scouring day in the North – and the stone floor of the kitchen was undergoing a thorough polishing. In the next house which I entered, I found in the loom garret only a young man of about eighteen, a smart intelligent lad. He was working at "greys", a coarse kind of silk stuff, which is printed and made into bandannas. "He could manufacture six cuts a week, and the price for each cut was 2s. 4½d. He did not, however, receive all he earned. He was an apprentice to the undertaker who rented the house. He had been bound for three years, and he now received 2s. 3d. of what he made. For the first two years of his apprenticeship he had received only one-half. Many of the undertakers tried to get apprentices bound for seven years, but people didn't like that. The work was terribly irregular, or it would not be bad work – but when folk was busy, it behoved them to save up money against when they had to go "play". He had been three months playing, and several times six, seven, and eight weeks. The trade was generally slackest towards midsummer. "What did the men do when they played?" "Why, they did not do no work." "How did they pass their time?" "Oh, different ways, according to fancy. They were a great deal in the streets. They took walks, and went to each other's houses, or anywhere. Some of them had dog-fights, but they were the lowest sort. Only the lowest sort had dog-fights in Macclesfield. There might be pigeon matches, but he had never heard much tell of them. As for himself, he liked to read and play the fiddle." "What did he think was the cause of these stagnations in the trade?" "Well, he had heard say as they were caused by over-production. More goods were made nor people wanted. Then the masters couldn't sell what they had on their shelves, and of course they didn't want for more, so the looms stood idle. It was a necessity. The weavers there about didn't eat very much flesh meat. Certainly, as a general thing, not every day. Some would have it though, whatever came of it. They would think the world couldn't go on if they hadn't flesh meat to dinner. But a great lot lived poor in the town. A great lot, too, were fond of fine clothes, particularly the young women, and they would have their backs gay although their bellies pinched for it."

The Macclesfield Mechanics' Institute is a flourishing establishment. The great majority of the members are silk weavers. They have recently been making considerable additions to the building, and they have a library containing more than 2,000 volumes. The secretary spoke in high terms of the general standard of intelligence of the silk population. Of their marked superiority in appearance to their neighbours, the cotton workers, there can be no doubt. The nature of their occupation is not only more conducive to personal cleanliness, but to the development of those minor symbols of health which are to be found in the presence of clear skins, bright eyes, and good complexions. One is inclined to wonder at the co-existence of comparatively, so low a rate of wages, with the outward evidences of, comparatively, so fair a state of social comfort. And wages, I am informed, are likely to sink even still further. The weavers living in remote country districts are gradually absorbing much of the work which used to be exclusively performed in Macclesfield.

MIDDLETON

SOMEWHAT MORE than five miles from Manchester, and mid-way upon the high road to Rochdale, lies, in a pleasant hollow, surrounded by ridging hills, and watered by the stream of the Irk, the ancient village of Middleton. Although near the centre of the charmed circle within which the steam-engine, the three-decked mule, and the power loom are alone potent, and almost as it were beneath the heel of the cotton capital – still the prevailing spirit of the region has passed but lightly over Middleton. Standing on the gravestone-clad hill, beneath the antique belfry of the Norman church, you see in your immediate neighbourhood but a few scattered stragglers from the host of tall chimneys which muster on the horizon. Beneath you, perched upon gardened banks or nestling in petty ravines, lie the scattered streets of an old-fashioned village, the high-gabled and irregular tenements built of wood which was leafy three centuries ago, interspersed with ranges of modern red-brick two-storied cottages. There is a gas-work rising, spick and span new, close to where the long grass is waving on the ruins of a brave hall; and a Manchester omnibus stands at the door of a tavern which may have seen the esquire ride forth to fly his hawks. There is nothing of the suburban character about Middleton. The citizens of Manchester do not resort there. The place has a stamp of its own. Some of the oldest and purest blood of the Lancashire yeoman keeps its current still unmixed by the hearths of this village. Needwood and Charnwood sent forth no tougher bows nor longer shafts than twanged along the banks of the Irk, and amid the coppices of Birtle and Ashworth. On the northern window of the church transept are emblazoned the effigies of the

Middleton Archers, who, like Hubert's grandsire, drew good bows, not indeed at Hastings, but on Flodden Edge. There, upon the coloured glass, march, like the merry men of Robin Hood, the staunch Middleton Archers, all of a row, with their long light Saxon hair, and their retainers' liveries of blue. Each carries his unslung bow upon his shoulder; over each bow is painted, in antique letters, the name of its owner, and every one of these names is still borne by an inhabitant of Middleton. It was curious, indeed, after the multitude of brown bricken Sions, and Ebenezers, and Bethesdas, to which I have lately been accustomed, to find myself standing upon the brazen memorials of buried Crusaders, amid mullions and *quatrefeuils*, carved by Norman chisels, and beneath mouldering standards and rusty spears, which were probably shaken and couched in the wars of the Roses. And in moral as well as physical attributes is the stamp of the old age strong upon this Lancastrian hamlet. A great deal of what was generally believed in England under the Tudors is believed in Middleton and its neighbourhood to this day. Indeed, says the courteous and accomplished Rector, "the people are but too apt to disbelieve what they ought to believe, and to believe what they ought to disbelieve." The fortune-teller abounds, and his oracles are as gospel. The astrologer still casts nativities and projects schemes, and the culler of simples is careful to pluck his herbs only during the waxing of the moon. Upon a dead wall I saw a placard announcing that the "Sacred Drama of Joseph and his Brethren" would be performed by certain Sunday-school pupils. Most unfortunately the date of the representation was past, or I would have astonished you by a critique upon something in the nature of a mediaeval mystery seriously enacted almost amid the smoke of modern Manchester.

Middleton Church, 1844

From what I have stated the reader will be prepared for a population pursuing some distinct and ungregarious species of occupation. He is in the right. The "folk o' Middleton", to use their own vernacular, are almost all silk handloom weavers, pursuing their craft in their own houses, preserving an independent and individual tone of character, intermarrying to the extent of breeding scrofulous disease – clannishness and prejudiced and peculiar as all such septs are – keeping up even amid their looms a great degree of the rural and patriarchal tone of by-gone times – a few of them handling the plough and the hoe as well as the shuttle and the winding-wheel and the entire community great favourers of the old English manly sports. "When the Hopwood hounds pass the village (says the Rev. Mr. Dunsford, the rector), there is always a goodly train of sportsmen, on foot, in attendance."

On my arrival in the village I inquired where I could best see the weavers at their work, and was directed to the "club-houses." Do not imagine however a satin-weaving Pall Mall. Turning from the high road, which is also the main street, I climbed a roughly-paved lane skirted by common-place mean houses, some of them little shops, and presently I heard on all sides the rattle of the shuttle. Still the aspect of the place was half rural. Trees here and there bowered the cottages, and the noise of the flail mingled with that of the loom. The "club-houses" were a double row of two-storey cottages, constructed by an old club or building society, whence the name, and not dissimilar in general arrangement to those I have so often described as forming the operative homes of Manchester. They were reared upon the face of a steep hill, and the surface of the street between them being level, the ground-floors on the lower side of the way are unavoidably underground-floors. You descend them by means of a roughly-paved area, extending the whole length of the street. The general aspect of the place was certainly humble enough; and the day being a dismally wet one, everything looked cheerlessly sloppy. I entered a house at random; as usual, the street door was the parlour door, that is to say, the door of the parlour, and kitchen, and hall. Two apartments opened from the principal one, the small one to the back being a sort of scullery and store-room, piled up with dirty dishes and household utensils, waiting to be washed; the other, a room nearly, if not quite, as large as the dwelling chamber, was the "loom-shop," where business is conducted.

First, of the living room. It was a sort of country cousin to the same class of apartments in Manchester, furnished a good deal after the same fashion, in rather a rougher way, to be sure, but wanting the grime and smoke-dried air, and the close, hot smell of the town operatives' lodging. In the corners were niched the invariable cupboards. From the wall ticked the invariable clock; beside it hang little miniature-sized engravings in black frames. On the high chimney-piece were tiny pieces of nick-nackery, china and glittering ware, in the usual cottage style, and on each side of the fireplace hung the usual polished pot lids. There was good substantial furniture in the place; strong useful deal tables, an old-fashioned chest of drawers, chairs of different patterns – some of them antique, high-backed affairs, the wood carved into innumerable lumps – others like the ordinary Windsor pattern; and by the fireside the never-to-be-too-highly-honoured rocking-chair. The floor was stone-flagged, sanded, and clean; and I must not omit to mention that on either side of the grate stood excellent cooking ranges – a feature almost universal in the Middleton weavers' cottages. Altogether, the place was by no means uncomfortable, inspiring neither the idea of privation nor unwholesomeness. I was met on the threshold by a decently-dressed middle-aged woman, who ushered me into the loom-shop, where sat busy at his work her lord and master. The work-room boasted but an earthen floor, scratched and scraped by half a dozen cocks and hens, which were jerking their necks about beneath the mechanism of the four looms which the chamber contained. The loom arrangements were barbarously primitive. There was a hole scooped in the earth beneath the treddles, and the weaver sat, like the craftsman of Hindostan, half buried in the earth, which, however, seemed as dry as Sahara. The walls were fairly whitewashed; and the stretching oblong window, or rather range of windows separated from each other by a two or three inch broad strip of wall, furnished the "Long Light," already so often alluded to. Of the four looms in the apartment two were at work, one of them wrought by the husband, the other by the wife. Before the former, on the loom, was stretched a piece of blue satin – the rich texture of the stuff contrasting well with the rude woodwork in which extended that glossy mesh of purple threads. I had some difficulty in drawing this weaver into conversation. He was not sullen, but not intelligent. While I stood by his loom, his wife took her place at hers, and began to labour upon a piece of brown silk shot with blue.

The man lamented over the fall of wages. Twenty years ago he used to make twice as much as now. He didn't know how it was. He supposed it was the masters. They was hard on the poor man. They was very grievous in their 'batements. When the weaver carried his work home, the master or the agents wor very clever to see flaws in it. They wouldn't see none, not them, if they wor a selling it to a customer; trust 'em for that. And wages was failing still. For a piece he would have got twenty shillings and sixpence for eighteen months ago, he could hardly get sixteen shillings now. It wasn't so bad with some sorts of silks. It all depended on the fashions and the run there was in the market. It would take a very clever weaver to make 10s. a week as a general thing, but there wor some good pieces as paid well, if the weavers could get plenty of work at them. He wrought, himself, ten hours a day or twelve, just as he was in the humour – some days more nor other days. If he wor lazy beginning in a morning, he made up for it at night. Sometimes he stopped the loom and went for a walk – why not? I inquired whether the house belonged to him. No, he wished it did. A vast heap in them parts lived in their own houses – more nor in any town of Lancashire. The children (by the way – they were feeding the poultry with crumbs of bread left from the dinner table) – the children were just brought up to their father's trade. There was naught else for 'em to do."

The woman told me that she was weaving silk for which she was paid 6½ d. per yard, and she could make only two yards by a hard day's work.

In the next house I visited, the man – a stalwart well-looking fellow – had just taken a piece of silk off the loom and was folding it on the table. He had to carry it to Manchester to be paid for his work. I admired the beauty of the stuff. "Aye, aye, but there be always soom'mut to find fault wi' when I take it whoam, that they may bate me down." He worked long hours – just as long as any factory hours. If he didn't begin so soon in the morning he kept at it longer at night. He was independent in that way, however. "Yes, that wor soom'mut. They often wove in these parts till ten o'clock in the long winter nights. A good weaver couldn't make more nor 8s. or 9s. a week. There wor some sorts of odd work as paid far better – perhaps a dozen, or it might be fourteen shillings; but they had seldom such a price. Wages wor failing – that was over true. He thought it was the fault o' the machinery."

I said that they were not so ill off at Middleton as Spitalfields.

"Aye, aye; but it's a poor sort of work, and I dinna doubt but they want to banish silk weavers from Spitalfields. It's too low and too poor a life for the fine folks o' Lunnon."

I crossed the street and made my way into one of the lower situated houses. The general arrangements were nearly the same as those I have already described, in the first dwelling that I visited. In this house a stout, burly-looking fellow, with a decided Milesian look, was smoking at the ingle corner; and a gaunt, pale-looking, middle-aged woman was seated on a low stool, rocking her lean body backwards and forwards, and pulling away at a pipe with great gusto. In the work-room were four looms. A rather nice looking girl of fourteen was working one – a sallow, unshorn-lean man another. The latter was producing beautiful figured silk. He was paid for it 9d. per yard, and could weave three yards a day. The price within his recollection would have been 2s. a yard, "Wornt that enough to make a man bitter at his work?" For other sorts of silk 4d. a yard was paid, and he well remembered when it was 1s. 3d. What was the cause of this? "Lord! He didn't know; I ought to know better nor him." "Were there more people weaving now than when he was a boy?" "Aye, that there wor – twice as many."

I had several times asked whether there was any weaver among them whom they thought especially a clever man, and one who knew the history of the trade. Public opinion pointing with many fore-fingers to a certain door, I tapped thereat, and the latch was raised by a venerable old lady adorned with a pair of silver spectacles on her nose, and a pipe in her mouth; she looked somewhat like a nice indulgent grandmamma – she had such a kind old-fashioned face; but I could not help staring at it, for never in my life had I seen an elderly lady's countenance embellished at once with a pair of silver spectacles and a clay pipe. The master of the family was a very intelligent, chubby old man, with grey hair, a pair of twin spectacles, but no pipe. After ascertaining that I was "not in the trade," and that I knew as much about the secrets of "dents-and-shute" as about the mysteries of Eleusis, he made me extremely welcome, and we had a long gossip together. In his workroom stood four looms, one of them the invention of the celebrated weaver of Lyons.[1] When I entered the master of the house was instructing a girl in the management of the loom. He straightway left his pupil, and, having heard my errand, launched headforemost into a sea of silk-weaving reminiscences.

I shall not attempt to classify the topics which I found scribbled in my note-book. In conversation with working men it is almost impossible to keep them to the point, and perhaps a more vivid idea is given of the colloquy, and especially of the principal interlocutor, by putting on paper his chat, rambling and disjointed as it was uttered.

"Remember better times? That do I well. Twenty-six years ago we had 13d. a yard for what we have 3½d. now. It's the machinery – the machinery as has done it – for see that Jacquard, and the silk in it (there are many hundred Jacquards hereabouts) – well, the weaving of that silk used to be 3s. a yard. What is it now? Why, 1s. 3d. About thirty years ago we were mostly cotton weavers here-away. But the power looms flung us out of work, and we were nigh starved. Then, sir, there came gentlemen from Lunnon, from Spitalfields (of course, as you come from Lunnon, you know Spitalfields), and they took down silk here and they set us to work on it. We was very glad to get the chance. But the masters was

---

[1] Jacquard, whose loom wove intricate patterns and pictures.

using us to bate down the Spitalfields weavers. Some of them, sir, – the weavers I mean – came down here, but their old masters wouldn't employ, no, not never a man on them, because they would want their old wages and old rules. That was the way, sir, that silk weaving became so general here-away. Well, but we was soon served just as we had served the Spitalfields folk. There's a place called Leigh, not far from here, where there was then a heap of hand-loom weavers as wrought cottons and such like. Well, after some time, our masters didn't give us our due, and so we combined and had a strike. What did the masters do but took the work to Leigh from Middleton, just as they did from Spitalfields to Middleton, and the weavers at Leigh wrought at one ha'penny a yard less than we did. To be sure they was glad to get the work at almost any price. The wages are not very different now, but there are grievous and unjust abatements. The masters are some of them honourable good men – but some of them are very tyrannous. They were very tyrannous in this way at Leigh, and a committee of the weavers collected information as to abatements, and printed it in a book. (I have the pamphlet before me.) Very often, sir, there was one and-sixpence and two-and-sixpence unjustly "bated" out of a week's work. The poor people could not live under it. They couldn't."

At this point we adjourned to the parlour. Grandmamma, with the pipe, swept up the hearth. A nice tidy girl sat peeling apples, apparently for a pie. Another weaver, a sturdy, good-humoured looking fellow, flung himself into a cosy elbow chair, with his legs over the arms, and we resumed our talk somewhat in this fashion.

"What rent may you pay now for this house?"

"Seven pounds a year, and a good many folk pay six."

The room was comfortable, and comfortably and substantially furnished. In an open corner cupboard sparkled two antique silver salt-cellars. I am always glad to see such things in a poor man's house. They were possibly heir-looms. The old weaver resumed.

"Some folks live in their own houses but I don't. This better nor factory work? Ay, that it is. You see you keep your children at home about you, and you don't lose control over them. We live very friendly like. There be all sorts here, but we're good folk together. When the children are ten or twelve years old we put them to the loom, but we must attend them, you know, and teach them. It takes long to make them perfect in the trade."

"Perfect in the trade!" exclaimed he of the elbow chair, "there's naught on us perfect in the trade. We are all learning."

The *pater familias* gravely coincided, and went on. "There's many drawbacks to a weaver's work. Sometimes it takes a week to gate a loom" (prepare it for a web of particular fineness). "I heard say that in Spitalfields all that is done at the master's charge, but here we do it ourselves. How do we live? Well; there's not much flesh meat eaten. There would be a deal more if we could get it. But there's tay (the Lancaster peasant invariably pronounces the word more Hibernico), there's tay, and bread, and bootter – that's ready cooking."

"Tay!" interrupted the younger weaver; "hot water and a little sugar, ye mean. It's not tay."

"Well," resumed his elder; "in this family we only have an ounce of tay a week; but I'll just tell you how we live in homely Lancashire sort. Well, we have tay and bread and bootter morning and afternoon. At dinner we have potatoes and perhaps a little meat. Here's in this house a family of four or five, as it may be. Well, at the end of the week we buy two or three pounds of beef, and that's all the flesh meat we have till next week. So we make it into as many dinners as we can scheme. We cook may be half a pound at a time, to give the potatoes a flavour like. But what's that for eating? Why, my share at meal-times is not bigger nor my thumb. So I often throw it in and take a fried ingan [onion] and two or three drops of vinegar to relish the potatoes. That's about our general way of living. To be sure we may get a lift in spring time when the spring fashions come; but very often we've been getting into debt in the winter; and first, you know, we must keep our credit; and then there's clothes want renewing. Teetotallers here? Aye, there be a few on 'em; but we're all very moderate."

"We wouldn't be so very moderate if we could afford a little drink better," said the second weaver.

"I like my glass of ale myself," resumed the first, "and I like good company, and a good joke and soom'mut to laugh at, I do. I like to sing a song too." How the conversation turned round I do not remember; but the next entry I have upon my note-book is, that the old gentleman was fond not only of a good song, but that he was especially fond of reading the "Skootchings" which Cobbett[1] used to give to people he didn't like.

---

[1] William Cobbett (1783-1835), the Radical author and journalist whose *Political Register* enjoyed a huge sale among the working classes.

Then we got back to convivial matters, and so gradually to the subject of the morale of the village.

"We've got a rural police here. But, Lord! we haven't no more use for them nor you have for water in your boots. There's three policemen, and the devil a thing they have to do but to walk about with their hands in their pockets, like gentlemen. Why, they haven't had a job this three months; except, may-be, when a chap gets droonk-like. The sergeant, as they call him, thinks it's quite ridiculous. He says he never saw such people. If he offends one he offends all. We like each other so well, and we turn out after dinner and have a great talk about politics, and what they're doing in Lunnon, and smoke our pipes. We often have long discussions – we're great chaps for politics, and we just go into each other's houses and talk. I like to be idle myself sometimes – I dare say you do, too. Yes, of course you do. Well, then, when I feel idle, I go and walk about in the fields maybe, and work harder to make up for it after."

I quite regretted being obliged to tear myself from my garrulous friend, who, I doubt not, would have talked till midnight with very great pleasure.

The next weaver I saw I was introduced to by the worthy rector. He was a patriarch of the village – a fine-looking old man of eighty two – with the remains of a well-cut massive set of features and curling white hair. He was feeble, and at times wandered in his speech. His dame was still a stout hearty body, enjoying a green old age; and busily employed when we called in scouring the flagged floor with hearthstone, a bucket, and a mop. She must have seen seventy winters, but she worked as vigorously and spoke as briskly as a damsel in her teens; her white hair all the while streaming from under a narrow frilled calico nightcap – the ordinary head-dress of the Middleton matrons.

The patriarch sat before the fire and babbled of times present and past. "The first silk ever woven in Middleton was made into bandanna handkerchiefs. Sixty years ago and better he had woven such himself. Some folk farmed then – others wove cotton. After the bandannas came twills and sarsnets and satins. Wages were lower, much lower now, than in the old times."

"But did the people then live better than they do now?"

Somewhat to my surprise the old man said, "No, sir; no, they live better now. They have tay and coffee liken – (observe the lingering Saxon idiom) – tay and coffee *liken* the gentlefolk. I had coffee to my dinner this day, sir. They had porridge and milk then instead; and often, sir, they had to go three miles to fetch the milk. But still they didn't work in the old days as now. They ran after the hounds, or went a-shooting and a-sporting in the fields nigh three days a week, and many had farms and tilled them likewise."

"I suppose you drink a glass of beer sometimes," said the rector. "You can brew it yourselves, in this capital range."

At this the buxom old dame took up the word.

"Well, sir, some on 'em does, but others drink it at the hush houses – that is, sir, the places where they keep it withouten being licensed. But we have naught to say to such like. Oh, there's a much drinkin' – too much – folk com round door by door and ask, 'Will we buy a knife?' and if we say, 'Aye,' why, then, they out with a bottle of smuggled whisky and sells it. That's the knife, sir."

Leaving the octogenarian and his dame, Mr. Dunsford said he would show me a house built by an industrious and intelligent weaver, entirely out of his own savings – a house which, in the phraseology of the district, "all came through the eye of the shuttle". We crossed the Irk by a slippery wooden bridge. "That," said my companion, "that is, for its size, about the hardest worked brook in England." There had been many hours of heavy rain, and the flood was rushing turbulent and strong. It looks as if it had been a likely trout stream long ago, but the gudgeon is now the only tenant of its waters. Verify the gudgeon must be a long-enduring fish – patient of foul things as an ichthyologic Job. The house we went to see was a neat and substantial cottage, built on the summit of a steep garden-planted bank. The industrious family who dwelt in it were its architects, and a snugger kitchen or a neater parlour, in a small way, might not easily be found. Over the dresser was ranged a fair collection of useful books.

To the Rev. Mr. Dunsford I am indebted for some interesting notices of the "Middleton folk", touching matters on which a stranger could not, during a hurried visit, well gain information for himself. The people are very generally careless and indifferent about the education of themselves or their children, taking the latter from school as soon as they can be useful at the loom. Writing is the attainment which they must prize, and most excel in. The art is a mechanical one, and Mr. Dunsford is convinced that the symmetrical order and due slope of the threads constantly stretching before their eyes exercise no little effect in producing good penmen from amongst weavers. The young people marry early, and although long periods of betrothal are common, they almost invariably take each other for better for worse without a stick of furniture or a shilling of saved money. The bride and bridegroom then go to live in the house of the parents of one of them; or frequently one takes his or her meals and remains during the day with his or her own friends; the other doing the same thing at another house, and the couple coming together again in the evening. During this time they pay for "loom room", or in other words, hire a loom a piece, and pay also for their board. Sometimes the father thus becomes a sort of capitalist – letting out, in a large family of sons and daughters, as many as half-a-dozen looms. Generally, by the time the first child is born, the young couple have saved something towards furnishing a dwelling for themselves – and that the more often inasmuch as their notions of setting up housekeeping are very modest. If they have a bed, a chest of drawers, and a corner cupboard they think that in all the essentials of furniture they are set up. The bedrooms are very generally, neat, clean, and tidy, beyond what might be looked for. The hand-loom system here appears, so far as family is concerned, to exercise exactly the opposite effect of the factory system. The Middleton weaver keeps not only his sons and daughters, but often his sons and daughters in law, long about him; while the children who are too young, and sometimes the adults who are too old for the heavy labour of the loom, turn the winding wheel, and prepare the glistening silk for the frame. They are great politicians, the good folks of Middleton, and occasionally given to lazy fits, during which smoking, sauntering, and chatting listlessly are the amusements most in vogue. The women very frequently smoke, but it is always with some pseudo-medical excuse. They feel a "rising" or a "sinking", or a headache, or a toothache, or any ache, or no ache at all. A curious indication of the prevailing shade or radical politics in the village is afforded by the parish register, the people having a fancy for christening their children after the hero of the minute. Thus, a generation or so back, Henry Hunts were as common as blackberries – a crop of Feargus O'Connors replaced them – and latterly they have a few green sprouts labelled Ernest Jones.[1] A very small proportion of the weavers only labour in the fields; but in many farmhouses around there are looms which the women work during the long winter evenings. The Spitalfields hobby of pigeon fancying is not uncommon, particularly among the young men; and pigeon matches, which give rise to a good deal of gambling, are frequent. The birds are taken some miles away, and then flown back to their homes. Apropos of the betting propensity, there was a bagatelle table in the quiet tavern where the omnibus from Manchester deposited me, above which was inscribed the following naive and ingeniously-worded proclamation: "No gaming allowed on this board. Any person having a wager or wagers on this board, the landlord shall seize it, and spend it in liquor."

I mentioned to Mr. Dunsford the complaints which I had heard of the masters being grievously tyrannical in abating the nominal wages given, on account of alleged imperfections in the work. Most of these stories, he said, like other stories, had two sides to them. He had known weavers work for years for a firm

---

[1] Henry Hunt (1773-1835), Radical orator and demagogue, who was imprisoned after Peterloo. Feargus O'Connor (1794-1855) and Ernest Jones (1819-1868) were Chartist leaders. O'Connor founded the *Northern Star* which, in the early 1840s, regularly printed lists of 'infant patriots' who had been named after the 'Lion of Freedom'.

without any abatement being made, or at least any that was not admittedly just. Many of the abatements, so called, were fines for broken contracts for work not being finished at the stipulated time. Still he did not doubt but there were often cases of real hardship in the system – cases in which shabby and screwing agents sought, by extreme ingenuity in finding or fancying flaws, to bate down the fair price of the work. In the pamphlet published by the Leigh weavers' committee upon the subject, one fact most damning to the masters, if true, is broadly asserted – viz., that the weavers who are abated the most, and who, consequently, were the abatements justly made, must be the worst workmen, received by far the greatest share of labour from the employers. Many of the cases reported by the committee in question seem harsh and cruel to the last degree. As regards the amount of these abatements, I may mention, quoting at random from a great mass of tabular statistics, that out of £265 10s. 8d. of wages nominally earned by 171 weavers, £45 12s. 3d. was abated on account of real or alleged imperfections in the fabric, being an average of 5s. 4d. clipped from each man's pay.

By the time I had completed my tour of inspection lights were gleaming from the "loom shops", and in the wood-roofed market place gas jets flared amid the meat, and on the eager faces of chaffering customers. Two Manchester omnibuses, each with three horses, and an indefatigable horn-blowing conductor, stood at different inn doors, and I naturally selected the lightest laden. Although the rain was coming down in bucketfulls, and the interior of the vehicle I had chosen was all but empty, the other was thronged outside and in. I mentioned the matter to my only *compagnon de voyage*. "Oh," he said, "you don't know how queer they are, the weaver folk of Middleton. They have a line of omnibuses belonging to a man they like, and won't go in the other people's buses not if you paid them; they'd walk through all this rain and dirt to Manchester first. Sometimes they hoot the people who ride in t'other bus, and if we were each of us Middleton tradesmen, and to be seen where we are, why we'd never sell another ha'porth to a weaver of them all!"

A Manchester horse bus of later years

SADDLEWORTH

THE NAME of Saddleworth is applied to a range of wild and hilly country, about seven miles long and five broad, lying on the western confines of Yorkshire, and including one spot from which a walk of ten minutes will carry the visitor across the boundaries of four counties, into Lancashire, Cheshire, Derbyshire, and Yorkshire. To all intents and purposes, however, Saddleworth lies in the latter county – its heathery hills and deep valleys dividing the woollen from the cotton cities and being themselves peopled by a hardy, industrious, and primitive race, engaged in the manufacture of flannel and cloth sometimes in mills, sometimes by their own hearths – in which latter case the business of a dairy farmer is often added to that of a manufacturer, and the same hands ply the shuttle and milk the cows. Saddleworth is now intersected by the Leeds and Huddersfield Railway,[1] and, as a consequence, is beginning to lose much of those primitive characteristics for which it was long renowned. Until recently there was no regular means of transit from many of its valleys to the more open parts of the country. Goods were conveyed by the Manchester and Huddersfield Canal; and many a small manufacturer and comfortable farmer grew grey amid the hills, without having ever journeyed further than Oldham and Stalybridge on the one hand, and perhaps Huddersfield, or at the furthest Leeds, upon the other. The rail has, however, thrown open the wilds of Saddleworth to the

---

[1] The Huddersfield to Stalybridge section of the Leeds, Dewsbury and Manchester Railway was opened on August 1, 1849.

world. Mills, driven by water and steam, are rising on every hand, and the old-fashioned domestic industry carried on in the field and the loom-shop is gradually dying away.

I entered Yorkshire by way of Oldham. To some extent the domain of cotton seems to be invading that of wool, for, as my vehicle slowly toiled up the steep ascents of the many ribs which branch from the "backbone of England", the driver pointed out to me several old woollen-mills which are now cotton factories. Leaving the straggling streets and abounding tall chimneys of Oldham behind, we enter a bleak, hilly country, high, naked, and sterile. All around rise great lumpish ridges of hill, divided by loosely piled walls into cold-looking pasture fields, and clothed here and there with substantial stone-built cottages. The agricultural labour requisite hereabouts is light; but the few labourers are well off, making from 12s. to 15s. a week. We passed several of the poor Oldham besom makers, returning from the moors with vast bundles of dripping "ling" upon their backs; and at length, after a tedious ascent, attained a bare, wild summit, from whence bursts upon the view one of the finest panoramas of hill and valley to be found in England. Beneath you opens out a stretching vista of irregularly-running glens, hemmed in by bristling ranges of heather or fir-clad hills. Here slopes pleasantly to the sun a fair expanse of green pasture – there runs a ridge, grey with rock or purple with heather. The eye wanders over clumps of oak and through straggling woods of sombre fir – from cottage to cottage, and hamlet to hamlet, and mill to mill – the former often perched high upon the hills, where the green of the pasture begins to give place to the brown sterility of moss and moor, and the latter invariably nestled in the very bottom of the glen, each beside its lakelet of clear water, dammed up from the rapid stream of the Tame. It was a wild, stormy morning, with lowering clouds, now breaking, now gathering before the strong wind, which drove great masses of whirring vapour along the high mountain ridges, lashing the ground at intervals with such rattling bursts of hail and rain as only fall among the hills – and anon lulling, while a bright sun gleamed forth, lighting up the blue correys of the hills, flooding with its radiance the great belts of fertile green, and shining bright upon the dripping surface of grey sloping rocks.

All around – hill and glen, oaken coppice and fir wood, green pasture and healthy ridge – is Saddleworth.

Before proceeding to notice in detail the physical and social condition of the woolworkers of Yorkshire, it will tend to the clearer understanding of much of what I have to say, if, at the outset, I succinctly describe the general process of manufacture, which, in many instances, is performed from beginning to end in mills, and which is occasionally carried on partly in mills, partly in the homes of the workmen.

The raw material having been unpacked from the bales in which it arrives, is delivered over to the sorters. The duty of these men is to pick out and arrange the different classes and qualities of the wool, according to the length and fineness of the fabric. Their labour can only be performed by daylight, and their wages of course vary not only with the season, but with the different classes of raw material submitted to their manipulation – a mill manufacturing fine broad cloth needs more expert judges of the woof than one producing the coarser and inferior stuffs. Thus in a mill in Saddleworth manufacturing the blanketing which is used in certain parts of cotton machinery, the sorters earn from 15s. to 20s. weekly. In a mill in Huddersfield producing the finest cloth, the same class of workmen can make about 25s. a week in winter, and 27s. in summer. The next operation is one requiring merely unskilled labour, and is generally entrusted to women. It consists simply of picking the impurities out of the wool, and is paid for at about the rate of 1½d. per lb. The filthiest sort of woof is sometimes sent to the gaols to be picked, where the operation is performed for about 1d. per lb. In the vicinity of the country mills superannuated old women frequently earn 2s. or 3s. a week by picking. In the towns the process is performed in the mills, and an active hand may make from 6s. to 7s. a week by the operation. After being sorted and picked, the wool undergoes a series of washing, and sometimes of dyeing operations, according to the intended colour of the stuff into which it is to be wrought. As is more or less the case in all processes of the kind, the rooms in which they are carried on reek with the steam of hot water and the smells of melting dye stuffs. Some of the dyes used for fancy coloured goods are exceedingly unhealthy. A foreman in a mill at Huddersfield told me that he had frequently helped to carry out workmen who had fainted amid the stench. As a general rule, however, the emanations from the vat do not appear to exercise any particularly injurious effect upon the workmen, who are moreover a good deal in the open air. Dyers and washers make from 16s. to 18s. a week.

We now come to the first of the operations having reference to the preparation of the fibre. This is exactly analogous to the stage of cotton manufacture performed by the "devil" – the machine which tears the wool to pieces being termed the "willow". There is a little, but not much, dust and flying fibre evolved by the process. The wool, it will be observed, has been previously in the dyeing-vat, and during the next few stages of the manufacture the faces and hands of the workpeople assume much the same tint as will be exhibited by the cloth which they are preparing. The willow requires but a single attendant – generally a boy – who feeds it with the coarse material, and bears to the carding machine the torn and softened filaments. His wages may average from 6s. to 7s. per week. The woollen carding machine differs materially from that used for cotton – the "cards" produced by the former being rolled out sideways from the implement in distinct portions, each about a yard long, and forming, as it were, rope-like cylinders of woollen fibres. The feeder of the carding-machine – a boy or girl – earns about as much as the feeder of the willow. It is now the turn of the "slubber" to play his part. The duty of this workman is, by means of his slubbing frame – an apparatus somewhat like a spinning mule – to draw out the thick "cards" into slender threads. Each slubber is attended by two piecers, whose duty it is to renew the products of the carding machine as the slubbing frame successively exhausts them. This office is anything but a sinecure, as the slubbing frame draws out into yarn the cards as fast as the piecer can supply them. The slubber, who is always a man, can make from 18s. to 20s. a week. The piecers, who are often his children, have from 4s. 6d. to 6s. each. The process just described is exactly analogous to "drawing" in the manufacture of cotton. The wool having now been converted into yarn, has next to be spun. This operation is very similar to the same process in the cotton trade, but as it is not held to require the same zealous watchfulness, or the same delicacy of manipulation, the wages paid are considerably less, few or no woollen spinners making more than £1 per week. In some mills, mules similar to the self-actors of Lancashire are being introduced, attended to only by young persons, who may make from 11s. to 14s. a week, and superintended by a man, who has frequently two or more rooms under his charge. In other cases, each spinner has two mules to attend to, with one or more piecers to each, according to the number of spindles. The thread having been thus prepared, is now taken to the loom. For plain stuffs the shuttle is generally driven by steam, but in the case of many kinds of cloth, and of all kinds of fancy goods, handloom-weaving is preferred, if indeed it be not absolutely necessary. The average earnings of power-loom weavers may be stated at 12s. a week. They are sometimes men and sometimes women, and each weaver has, as a general rule, charge of two looms. The appearance of a cloth-weaving room is very different from that of a cotton "shed". The looms are larger, heavier, and clumsier in appearance, and the shuttle traverses the twelve or fourteen feet, which it has frequently to cover, with a far more deliberate motion than the glancing jerks of the cotton shuttle, flying through the fast growing webs of calico. The stuff having been woven, is subjected to the action of steaming hot water and the "fulling-hammers" which cause it to shrivel up almost to one half of its former dimensions. The wages earned by the artisans who labour in the steaming atmosphere of the fulling mill are from 18s. to 21s. The next process is exclusively performed by women. It is called "birling," and consists of picking out of the cloth, with a sort of tweezers, all the little knots and inequalities which may be apparent upon the face of the fabric. In the country, this operation is very generally performed at home. In towns, it is executed in the mills, the cloth being spread upon a wooden frame placed at an obtuse angle to the window, and three or four women, closely jammed together, being seated on benches before each frame. This is almost the only department of the trade in which married women are extensively employed away from their homes. In the birling room of a Huddersfield mill, I heard more giggling, and saw more symptoms denoting a relaxed state of discipline, than I had previously observed in any department in any of the textile industries. It was clear, from the atmosphere, that some of the women had been smoking, but the pipes were, of course, instantly smuggled away on our entrance. The cloth having been "birled", now undergoes a variety of operations included in the general term "finishing", the object being to render the surface as velvety smooth as possible, and to obtain that beautiful glossy face for which broad-cloth is remarkable. Men and boys are employed in these operations. The wages of the former may range from 18s. to 20s., and those of the latter from 5s. to 7s. It was the introduction of improved machinery in one of the operations under question – that of cutting smooth the face of the cloth – which produced the Luddite outbreak. In stating the general wages paid for the finishing processes, I ought not to omit that the "hot-pressers" are highly paid, their wages often amounting to 30s. a week.

I have thus sketched in general terms the process of woollen manufacture in its principal phases. He who sees a woollen mill preparing plain or slightly coloured stuffs will have a very different opinion of the cleanliness and pleasantness of the operation from the visitor who watches the stages in the production of broad cloth. When the wool is dyed of a deep colour previously to being carded, slubbed, and spun, the aspect of the mill and of the workpeople is grimy and filthy in the extreme, and the atmosphere of the various rooms is more or less charged with sickly-smelling odours produced by the dye-stuffs. Mills manufacturing the lighter and coarser species of stuffs are, on the contrary, clean-looking and agreeable to all the senses. In none of the rooms where the textile operations are being performed is any particular degree of heat required. In the dyeing and some of the finishing operations alone the temperature is necessarily high.

The first woollen mill which I inspected was that belonging to the Messrs. Whitehead,[1] in Saddleworth. It is a country factory, beautifully situated in the deep cleft of a wooded glen, and scattered round it are the cottages of the workpeople. As is generally the case with respect to country mills, the average rate of wages is somewhat below that paid in towns, from which the foregoing estimate has been constructed. The Messrs. Whitehead send their Buenos Ayres wool to be picked in the prisons of Manchester, that species of raw material being so coarse and dirty that it is difficult to find free labourers to meddle with it. A great deal of the ordinary picking is, however, done by the women in their cottages in the neighbourhood. The Messrs. Whitehead also put out their "birling", and many married women make a practice of birling a sufficient quantity to pay their rents, devoting the rest of their time to household duties. The domestic manufacture in this part of Saddleworth, which nearly adjoins the cotton districts, is fast dying away, and large old-fashioned houses attached to small farms

---

[1] The Royal George Mills in the valley of the River Tame, Greenfield.

are now being let at one-half and one-third the rents they formerly produced.

One interesting branch of the Messrs. Whitehead's manufacture is the construction of flags. They dye, spin, and weave the bunting which is cut into proper pattern, and sewn together either in their mill or in the cottages around. The flag makers are exclusively women. Although the industry is one principally carried on in seaport towns – the wives and widows of sailors being frequently the persons employed – there is many a yard of bunting manufactured amid the hills of Yorkshire by people who never saw a ship or the ocean. It seemed strange so far inland to come upon a room hung with gaily tinted bunting, the forms and colours of ensigns and Union Jacks painted upon the tables, and collections of the patterns of national and signal standards displayed upon the walls. The bunting, after being cut into due form, is firmly sewn together. And there is a regular fixed scale of prices paid to the work-women for the different descriptions of flags. For a scarlet ensign, five yards long, with the Jack in the corner, 2s. 1d. is paid; for an ensign of four yards, 1s. 1d.; for a Union Jack of four yards, 2s. A good sewer can make at this work from 8s. to 10s. a week. They seldom commence operations until eight a.m. The best workmen in the Messrs. Whitehead's establishment earned the week before my visit 10s. 10d., and the week before that 12s. 3d. A great number of flags are, however, manufactured at the homes of married women, who give part of their time to this species of industry. On referring to their books, the Messrs. Whitehead informed me that 3s. might be the average earnings of a workwoman of this class. Selecting at random a name, I found that the owner had in three weeks earned respectively 3s. 10d., 3s. 1d., and 3s. 8d.

From the mill I proceeded to visit some of the cottages of the workpeople. Without a single exception, I found them neat, warm, comfortable and clean. They consisted almost universally of a common room, serving as a parlour and kitchen, a scullery behind it, and two or more bedrooms upstairs. The main rooms were, I think, as a general rule, larger than those I have lately been accustomed to see. The floors were stone flagged, nicely sanded. Samplers and pictures uniformly ornamented the walls, and the furniture was massive and old-fashioned; the chairs with rush bottoms, and high well-polished backs. One characteristic feature of these cottages was universal. It consisted of a sort of net stretched under the ceiling, and filled with crisp oat cakes. These formerly constituted almost the only bread consumed in the district, but home-baked wheaten loaves are now coming into general use. Indeed almost every family in Saddleworth bakes its own bread and brews its own ale – a capital nutty flavoured beverage it is. The composition of the oat cakes is, however, held to require a peculiar genius, and when a matron gets a reputation in that way, she frequently bakes for half a village. In the first cottage I entered I found a rosy-cheeked girl occupied in "birling". Her father worked in the mill; her mother had her household to attend to, and did a little "birling" besides. The matron, upon her appearance, informed me that the house had five rooms, and that the weekly rent which they paid for it was 3s. 4d. The girl could by devoting the whole of her time to the work, make 7s. or 8s. per week by "birling". It was common for married women to birl enough to pay the rent, which they could do, and get ample time to attend to their families. Very few married women worked in the mills. They found no difficulty in getting as much work as they wanted at home. In the second house which I saw there were also five rooms, and the rent 3s. 1d. per week. Besides this, the occupants paid 6d. a week for gas, which they could keep alight until half-after ten, and on Saturdays and Sundays as long as they pleased. The woman of the house was a fine, fat, hearty-looking dame of sixty, the very picture of health and matronly enjoyment. There was a bed, with curtains, in a corner of the room. Who the occupant was I do not know – he did not think proper to show himself, but ever and anon a voice from amid the blankets joined vigorously in the conversation. The old lady corroborated the statement I had heard as to the small proportion of married women who preferred working in the mills to "birling" at home. The use of oat cake, she said, was gradually decreasing and she produced a substantial home-made wheaten loaf as a specimen of the bread coming into favour. She could remember when the people ate nothing but oat cakes. These were then made four times as thick as now. The people used to eat a great deal of cheese. Indeed, they used to live on cheese, oat cake, porridge, and butter milk, but nowadays nothing but tea and coffee would do for them. They took a great deal of porridge yet, however, for breakfast; but generally they had some meat for dinner, perhaps some bacon, perhaps some beef. At all events, they had plenty of porridge and bread and potatoes. The price of meat was a little dearer than when she was a girl. Good mutton could not be had now under 6d. a lb., but she thought, on the whole, that people lived just as well now as they did forty years ago.

At one end of a straggling village, called Upper Mill, I entered a small factory in which carding and slubbing are performed. The place was rudely and clumsily built; the stone stairs were dirty, and the joists and beams of the house bare and exposed. In the principal room I got into conversation with the slubber, who stopped his machine to give me what information he could. His wages averaged about 18s. a week. He worked ten hours a day. The little piecer was his daughter, and her wages were 4s. 2½d. Another of his daughters worked under his eye as a carding feeder. Her wages were 5s. 10d. The united earnings of his family were better than 30s. a week, and of course they lived pretty comfortably. He paid only 2s. 3d. a week for a very decent cottage with a buttery (the old word is still in use in Saddleworth), a kitchen, and two bedrooms. For breakfast, they had all porridge and milk, and for dinner they had generally a little meat, with bread and potatoes, and home-brewed beer. His wife did nothing save her household work. The carding-feeder, an intelligent girl about 16 years of age, observed that the price of provisions had very much fallen within the last two years. Meat, which used to be 7d. per pound, could now be had for 6d., and flour, which used to be 3s. per stone of 12 lbs. might now be bought for 1s. 10d. Tea and coffee were also cheaper. They generally bought a quarter of a pound of tea for 15d. weekly, and one pound of coffee for 1s. These groceries were purchased at Mossley, a small town not far from Stalybridge, to which one of the family went weekly for the purpose. If they were to buy tea and coffee at Upper Mill they would have to pay 18d. and 14d. for it respectively, instead of 15d. and 1s., and they would not get such a good article for the higher as they now did for the lower price.

I had the good luck to light upon a courteous gentleman, a manufacturer at Upper Mill, who was born and bred in the district, and who understands the people and their habits thoroughly. In the mill owned by this gentleman no adult male receives less than 15s. a week, and many young men, from 16 years of age to 20, earn between 12s. and 14s. He gives out a good deal of birling to be performed by the married women at their homes, and pays them 4s., 5s., and 6s. a week for their work. As a general thing, he thought the weavers in mills might earn about 14s. a week, the slubbers about 18s., and the spinners from 18s. to 20s. There was no child employed by him earning less than 3s. Some children had 3s. 6d., others 4s., others 5s. The process of "finishing" in the cloth trade paid well. Boys of twelve years of age in his mill were making 10s. and 11s. a week, and the principal hands had from £1 1s. to 30s.

Understanding that the "hand spinning jenny" is still extensively used in Saddleworth, I requested my informant to take me where I could see this, to our present notions, primitive instrument at work. I found that there were plenty going all round us. The wool is generally willowed, carded, and slubbed in the mills. The domestic manufacturers then carry the yarns home, spin them upon the hand jennies, and weave them in the same apartment.

"Do you see," said my conductor, "that jolly looking old fellow, loading a horse with a pack of goods? Well, he's rather a good specimen of the domestic manufacturers of Saddleworth. I warrant you he's worth not less than two or three thousand pounds. We'll go and see his place."

The general appearance of the village, I should say, is that of a straggling, yet substantially-built hamlet – the oblong ranges of windows running along beneath the eaves of many of the houses, denoting the nature of the occupation carried on within them. Sometimes they stand alone, backed by steep banks of grass and stunted trees; sometimes they are clustered together with narrow courts and passages leading from the highway. Up one of these courts we proceeded, and after passing through one of the usual parlour kitchens, ascended a ladder to the work-room. Here were two looms and two hand-jennies; each of the latter may have had about forty spindles. They are worked upon the general principle of the power mule – the muscle of the operative, however, supplying the place of the steam engine. In fact, the whole machine looks somewhat like a toy power mule.

A spinning jenny, 1852

One of the looms and one of the jennies only were at work when we entered, being urged respectively by a son and daughter of the old proprietor, who however speedily made his appearance, and took his place at the vacant jenny. The operator, with this machine, performs the whole of the work acting as piecer as well as spinner.

The labour, however, cannot be called severe, for the travelling frame is exceedingly light, and a very weak arm is sufficient to propel it. The girl told me that she was making about 8s. a week. Before the introduction of power mules she could have made nearly twice as much; but wool spinning would soon be performed altogether by steam and machinery, because steam and machinery could do it much faster and much cheaper than men or women.[1] The weaver said he could sometimes make 15s. a week – that was when he got a good web; but the average with the cloth hand-loom weavers was considerably lower. Porridge and milk made the best of their fare, with butter-cakes and meat "when they could catch it". The workroom where these people wrought was airy, but not by any means particularly cleanly.

From this place we proceeded by a steep path up the hill side to a cluster of old-fashioned houses called Saddleworth Fold, and which were the first, or amongst the first, stone buildings erected in the district. They are occupied by several families, who are at once spinners, weavers, and farmers. The hamlet was a curious irregular clump of old-fashioned houses, looking as if they had been flung accidentally together up and down a little group of knolls. Over the small latticed windows were carved mullions of stone, and in a little garden grew a few box-wood trees, clipped into the quaint shapes which we associate with French and Dutch gardening. The man whose establishment we had come

---

[1] Spinning on jennies continued for many years in Saddleworth and two were used until the early years of the 20th century. See C. Aspin, *James Hargreaves and the Spinning Jenny*, Helmshore, 1964, p. 57. One machine is now in the Higher Mill Museum, Helmshore; the other in the (currently closed) Industrial Museum, Halifax.

to see was a splendid specimen of humanity – tall, stalwart, with a grip like a vice, and a back as upright as a pump-bolt, although he was between 70 and 80 years of age. We entered the principal room of his house; it was a chamber which a novelist would love to paint – so thoroughly, yet comfortably, old-fashioned, with its nicely-sanded floor, its great rough beams, hung with goodly flitches of bacon, its quaint latticed windows, its high mantel-piece, reaching almost to the roof, over the roaring coal fire, its ancient, yet strong and substantial furniture, the chests of drawers and cupboards of polished oak, and the chairs so low-seated and so high-backed. An old woman, the wife of the proprietor, sat by the chimney corner with a grandchild in her lap. Her daughter was engaged in some household work beside her. In this room the whole family, journeyman and all, took their meals together. Porridge and milk was the usual breakfast. For dinner they had potatoes and bacon, or sometimes beef, with plenty of oat bread; and for supper, "butter-cake", or porridge again. The old man had never travelled further than Derby. He had thought of going to London once, but his heart failed him, and he had given up the idea. He did not at all approve of the new-fangled mill system, and liked the old-fashioned way of joining weaving and farming much better. He could just remember the building of the newest house in Saddleworth Fold. He thought the seasons had somehow changed in Saddleworth, for snow never lay upon the ground as it used to do, and the scanty crops of oats here and there sown did not ripen so well. The daughter having in the meantime placed oat cake and milk before me, the patriarch observed that until he was twenty he had never tasted wheaten bread, except when his mother lay in. In the room above us were two or three looms, and as many spinning jennies. They produced flannel and doeskin. Weaving and spinning formed the chief occupation of his family – they attended to the cows, of which he had four, and to the dairy, in their leisure time. He paid his sons no regular wages, but gave them board, lodging, and clothing, and "anything reasonable" if they wanted to go to a hunt or a fair or "sooch-loike".

I may as well state here that the country weavers of Saddleworth are, like Nimrod, mighty hunters. Every third or fourth man keeps his beagle or his brace of beagles, and the gentlemen, who subscribe to the district hunt, pay the taxes on the dogs. There are no foxes in Saddleworth – the country, indeed, is too bare for them to pick up a living; but hares abound, and occasionally the people have "trail-hunts" – the quarry being a herring or a bit of rag dipped in oil dragged across the country by an active runner, with an hour's law. A few, but only a very few, pursue the sport on horseback – the weavers, who form the great majority of the hunt, trusting to their own sound lungs and well-strung sinews to keep within sight of the dogs. Even the discipline of the mills is as yet in many instances insufficient to check this inherent passion for the chase. My informant, himself a mill-owner, told me that he had recently arranged a hunt to try the mettle of some dogs from another part of Yorkshire against the native breed. He had tried to keep the matter as quiet as he could, but it somehow leaked out, and the result was that several mills were left standing, and that more than 500 carders, slubbers, spinners and weavers formed the field. The masters, however, are often too keen sportsmen themselves to grudge their hands an occasional holiday of the sort. The Saddleworth weavers must be excellent fellows to run. A year or two ago, a gentlemen, resident there, purchased a fox at Huddersfield and turned him loose at Upper Mill, a spot almost in the centre of the hills. There started on the trail upwards of 300 sportsmen on foot. Reynard led the chase nearly to Manchester, a distance of about 20 miles, and then doubled back almost to the place where he was unbagged, favouring his pursuers with an additional score of miles' amusement. Of the 300 starters, upwards of 25 were in at the death. My informant had reason to remember the chase, for it cost him the bursting of a blood-vessel. In passing through the little village of Dobcross I observed a quaint tavern sign, illustrative of the ruling passion. On the board was inscribed, "Hark to Bounty – Hark".

From Upper Mill I proceeded to a village called Delph, where there are only a very few mills, and round which is scattered a thick population of small farmers and hand-loom weavers. The cottages of many of these people are perched far up among the hills, on the very edge of the moors. As a general rule, the houses are inferior, both in construction and cleanliness, to those nearer the mills; and I should say, although the accounts I received were often most puzzlingly contradictory, that the run of wages is decidedly lower. In several of these remote dwellings I found beds of no inviting appearance in the loom room; and broken windows were often patched with old hats and dirty clothes. The hand-jenny spinners, when in employment, earn, as a pretty general rule, about 8s. a week. The weavers may and often do make 15s. and 17s. per week, but, taking the year round, and the good webs with the bad ones, 10s. in many parts of Yorkshire would be too high an average. As a general rule, the Saddleworth weavers seem to be better off than those upon the lower grounds round Huddersfield and

Halifax. Among the hills dairy farms are very common; but the nearer we get to large towns the more rare does the union of occupations become. High up on the hill side above Delph I counted from one point of view a couple of dozen cottages, in each of which the loom was going, and around each of which the kine were grazing. It was a glorious sunny afternoon, and amid the fields, and by the road side, the weavers with their wives and children were many of them stretching out their warps upon a rude apparatus of sticks to dry them in the genial air. The gay tinting of many of these outstretched meshes of thread, glancing along the green of hedges, or the cold grey of stone walls, made quite a feature in the landscape. The workpeople were very chatty and communicative. With two in particular I had long conversations, after which I accompanied them to their houses. The first was a slatternly place – one of those in which dirty beds lay unmade in the workshop. The weaver complained of the uncertain nature of his work, and spoke bitterly of the power-loom, which would, he was afraid, in the long run beat him and his comrades out of the field. Wages, within his own recollection, had sunk one-half. He lived upon potatoes, porridge, oatcake and milk, and meat "when he could catch it" – a common phrase hereabouts. Trade was not very brisk at present, but it was much better than it was, "because" wheat and meat were cheaper. I asked him whether dear bread and bad trade always came together. His answer was, "I never knowed it otherwise with the weavers. Look, sir, when everything to eat was terrible dear two years ago, what happened to us. Why, we could not get no work at no price, and all the weavers hereabouts that hadn't farms were forced to turn out and work at the railway tunnel under Stannidge.[1] If it wasn't for that, I don't know what would ha' becoom of us."

Another weaver, a very intelligent man – much more so indeed than most of his class, for he had travelled much, and been twice in America – gave me some curious information. He confirmed what the old man at Saddleworth Fold had stated, as to the non-ripening of oats sown now-a-days, and spoke sensibly enough about machinery. "Machinery," he said, "had been a great advantage to the weaver as long as it was pretty simple and cheap, for then he could use it for his own behoof." His mother had told him that in her younger days the distaff was the only drawing implement in Saddleworth. The carding was performed by the woman with a rude instrument placed upon their knees, and the old-fashioned wheel, with its single spindle, was the only spinning apparatus known. "Look, sir," he continued. "at that yarn. It was stretched out by the road side today. In those days it would have taken a dozen people, with a dozen of wheels, more than a week to spin it. Now my mistress can make it with the hand-jenny in two days and a half, and a power mule could spin it in a forenoon." He feared that it was but natural that the power mule would supplant the hand mule, just as the hand mule had supplanted the spinning wheel. It was during the time that machinery was in the medium state, when any industrious man could obtain it, that the weavers of Saddleworth flourished most. At one time he had paid a journeyman £35 a year besides his board, lodging, clothing, and washing, and they did not use, in those times, to work more than five or six hours a day.

---

[1] Standedge Tunnel, three miles 57 yards, was driven through the Pennines from Marsden to Diggle. For several years it was the longest tunnel in the world.

They were too often out following the hounds. Now his average wages were not above 10s. a week, although he could sometimes make nearer 20s. His wife worked the hand-jenny and could make, when in full work, about 15d. a day. Thirty years ago she could have easily earned 18s. a week. He kept a cow, and paid £7 10s. of rent for the requisite land. His family consumed most of the dairy produce, selling very little. The ordinary price of buttermilk was about 1d. for three quarts; of blue, or skim-milk, 1d. for three pints; and of new milk, about 2d. a quart. Milk of all kinds was sent down during the summer-time, in great quantities, by many of his neighbours, who kept donkeys to carry it, to Stalybridge, Oldham, and other cotton towns, where the factory hands consumed it as fast as it could be sent in.

Adverting to the work and food question, I asked him whether the high prices a year and a half ago had exercised much influence on his trade. He answered nearly as follows:

"Did they not, indeed! Why, when corn is very dear we have next to no trade at all. It stands to reason. The fabrics we make be mostly for the home market – the best and most nat'ral of all markets, sir; and if the poor people have to spend all they earn to pay for their food and to keep the roofs over them, why, they can't buy no good warm clothing. Two years ago flour was 3s. 6d. a stone, and oatmeal was 3s. 2d., and potatoes was selling as high as 2s. 6d. a score. Then, sir, there was next to no work. I was better off than many, but even in our house it was hard living I assure you; and a great lot of the weavers had to go to work along with t'navvies on the railroad."

I am happy to say that this honest man appeared to be in better case when I saw him. His house was beautifully clean, and his wife was preparing a comfortable stew for dinner. One of his children was recovering from scarlet fever, and two plump fowls were being boiled down to make chicken broth for the invalid. They had fifteen fowls, of which ten had been thus used up, and they expected every day to get a fresh supply of poultry.

Comfort such as this must, however, by no means be taken as the rule. The weavers in the upland districts who have farms, and those in the lower grounds who, although they possess no land, have got advantages of a particular class from the vicinity of the country mills – these two classes are generally decently off, and live wholesome and tolerably agreeable lives. But there are districts, principally in the neighbourhood of the large towns, where competition keeps the wages miserably low and where hard labour brings in but a hard and scanty subsistence.

A lady inspects the power looms, watched by a young mill
worker, 1844

Printed in the United Kingdom
by Lightning Source UK Ltd.
126438UK00001B/220-402/A